It has been a pleasure to work with David Tabatsky through his writing workshops for cancer patients and survivors at our annual Celebration of Life. His energy, commitment and expertise have enabled the participants to learn a valuable coping skill and begin to process their experiences in a new and often healing way.

—*Hester Hill Schnipper, program manager, Oncology Social Work,*
Beth Israel Deaconess Medical Center, Boston, MA

———

Write for Life will help a lot of people in recovery.

—*Dee Burrell, cancer survivor, author,*
Open Up the Door and Let Me In

———

When I was diagnosed, I would have loved to find a book like yours.

—*Mindy Greenstein, PhD, psycho-oncologist, author,*
The House on Crash Corner and Other Unavoidable Calamities

———

I am so happy that you have begun this venture.

—*Sean Swarner, cancer survivor, author,* Keep Climbing

———

If only I could hand our patients your book.

—*Pam Washek, founder, Wayland Angels*

———

Thank you for putting this book together.
—*Karen McCarty, cancer survivor, Big Apple Circus Clown Care*

———

Dear David Tabatsky,

Your cancer workshop in Seattle affected me deeply and lastingly. I feel it is crucial and much needed in our society. We are each inspired not only by your work but by your being, your obvious, kind, genuine, precisely guided intention. Simply thank you.

With gratitude,
Marty

David,

Thank you for coming all this way to help us and for teaching me that the most important thing you do is to listen. "The most essential thing in writing is to listen—to yourself and others." I will remember that. Like you said, listening is the hardest thing, but now that I know what to do to improve, I can focus on it. So thank you. I will remember to ask myself, "Why is something important? Look for the details there." Thank you for the lovely notes you wrote to my children in your book. I'm so glad I was able to meet you.

Warm regards,
Kim

Hi David,

Neal and I loved your advice on our book, to start the story at a critical decision point. We chose to start after my second relapse when I was offered another bone marrow transplant and decided instead to spend my remaining time enjoying life and seeking new experiences. This was last January and little did I know I would still be able to see baby pronghorns at Yellowstone, nesting puffins on the Oregon coast in summer, camp among the changing larch trees in the fall, and then still feel strong enough to be pulling my snowshoes out of the closet this winter. Speaking of which, I still have a few days before chemo so I better start packing for a quick snow excursion.

Take care,
Melissa

WRITE FOR LIFE

Books by David Tabatsky

Chicken Soup for the Soul's
THE CANCER BOOK: 101 Stories of Courage, Support & Love

THE WRIGHT CHOICE:
Your Family's Prescription for Healthy Eating,
Modern Fitness and Saving Money
(with Dr. Randy Wright)

THE INTELLIGENT DIVORCE: Because Your Kids Come First
(with Dr. Mark Banschick)

DEAR PRESIDENT OBAMA:
Letters of Hope from Children Across America
(with Bruce Kluger)

THE BOY BEHIND THE DOOR:
How Salomon Kool Escaped the Nazis
(Young Adult Historical Fiction)

WHAT'S COOL BERLIN
A Comedy Guide to Germany's Capital

Books Edited by David Tabatsky

THE RIGHT WORDS AT THE RIGHT TIME:
VOLUME TWO—YOUR TURN
(Consulting Editor for Marlo Thomas)

UNDER THE YARMULKE: Tales of Faith, Fun and Football
(Consulting Editor for Rabbi Solomon Schiff)

DO YOU DREAM IN COLOR?
Insights from a Girl Without Sight
(Consulting Editor for Laurie Rubin)

IT'S JUST A WORD:
Reclaiming Your Life Through Cancer—Beautifully!
(Elizabeth Bayer, Author)

SLIPPING REALITY
(Emily Beaver, Author)

FAMILIAR SHADOWS
(Bert Goolsby, Author)

Coming Soon:

BEAUTIFUL OLD DOGS:
A Loving Tribute to Our Senior Best Friends

WRITE FOR LIFE
*Communicating Your Way
Through Cancer*

David Tabatsky

ISBN—13: 978-1491237571
ISBN—10: 1491237570

Library of Congress Control Number: 2013915569

Visuals by Flash Rosenberg
Interior by 1106 Design
Cover by Bruce Kluger

For
Bob Lenox
and
Dani Palik

Contents

PART THREE—US:
It's All About Us
(The World at Large)

Foreword

Every once in a while, a book comes along that permeates my editorial insouciance and grabs hold of my heart. *Write for Life* is such a book. Written with compassion, humor, and a passionate belief that David can help somebody, this is a life-changing gift. Reading this book makes me feel happy to be alive and doing what I love: writing and coaching writers who have stories to tell.

When David asked me to write the foreword for this book, I asked, "Why me? I'm nobody." And herein lies the answer. We are all nobody. And we are all somebody. We are all equal as suffering human beings, all capable of joy, creativity, self-expression, and transcendence. Our nobody-ness is an illusion based on our feelings of separateness, isolation, and disconnectedness, from ourselves and others. It is a state of humility.

Ironically, it is that same question, Why me? that we scream out to the universe when trauma strikes us down and makes us feel helpless and defeated. The life-and-death wake-up call that grabs our souls and makes us shout, "I'm somebody. I want to live. I'm not done yet. I deserve a second chance." A third chance, and another, and another, until we feel we've fulfilled our greatest potential and made our dreams come true.

That's what *Write for Life* is about. At the simplest level, it's a companion, a mentor, a guide. David will run alongside you while you're running for your life. He will help you write to the bottom of your fear and panic, and guide you back up again. As my late acting teacher used to say, "Don't abdicate from the character's circumstances. Go out scared."

I am a survivor of many life-threatening traumas, some I'm willing to talk about. Some remain my secret. As a child, I survived seizures and scarlet fever. While my mother prayed and cried at my bedside, I hallucinated pink elephants dancing around my bed. They were there. I saw them. When David talks about the elephant in the room, I remember my pink elephants that sustained me, made me laugh, and gave me a second chance.

As a young adult, I survived a brutal assault—twice. I was left for dead for three days and endured three surgeries for my injuries, but the damage was permanent. The second assault, at gunpoint, had me begging for my life. Another second chance.

My biggest scare was cancer. Surgery saved my life from a constellation of precancerous cells. Imagine. A "constellation." A metaphor for stars had to be cut out of my body, adding insult to injury to my poetic soul. Again, another chance at life.

So as a member of the Survivors Club, I offer *Write for Life* to my fellow club members. With all due gratitude to the doctors who saved me, I confess that what really saved my life was writing. From early childhood, writing journals, poetry, plays, and stories kept "my pilot light going." David understands how vital this is—for your sanity and your soul's survival, in the most profound sense.

Writing is a way to stay alive while you're alive. It is the most direct route to your soul and its voice, your Self, your deepest will to live. For those who believe in the power of prayer, writing is like meditative prayer. It can be your salvation. It connects you irrevocably to who you are. It's another way to express your pain and, at the same time, release and separate yourself from your soul pain. Writing is a way to take care of yourself by loving yourself, as only you can do. It says yes to you, yes to your pain, yes to letting the pain pour out of you onto the page.

Another profound irony that David knows well is that staying connected to your true self through expressive writing keeps you "living in three tenses at once": the past, the present, and the future. They are all one state of being, of living in the moment, in the here and now. I learned that from my dad, who lived many years with Alzheimer's. He experienced everything, every memory, as the absolute present tense. As David says, through expressive writing, we have the chance, the capacity, "to get in touch with everything you're dealing with: the good, the bad, and the ugly."

Writing for your life is about telling the truth. Trust your feelings; they tell you the truth. When you are in communion with the truth, you can feel at one with the universe because you are self-expressing. Self-expression is our raison d'être as human beings. It is a fundamental human need—for reflection, introspection, and transcendence. It transports you from your dis-comfort zone to a new comfort zone, a new feeling of being "at home" with yourself in the universe. When you are in your new comfort zone, you will discover the other truth about your writing. You will know whether it is truly private for your own healing and comfort, or whether you want to share it with others.

Write for Life is for all the scared and the brave people who know that they are somebody, that their feelings, thoughts, lives, and stories are to be cherished by themselves, their loved ones, and the human community. They are writing for their lives and saying, "I am here. I am alive. I write. Therefore I am."

—Linda Roberts
August 2013

what if . . .

EXPRESS!

COURAGE

fear love

SUPPORT FAITH

Introduction

Every 23 seconds, someone in America is diagnosed with cancer. In an instant, fear and uncertainty take over. Everything comfortable and familiar suddenly feels out of control.

What if you began expressing yourself in writing, and that led you to communicate more effectively with your family, friends and doctors? What if writing relieved some of your stress and helped you feel more in control of your situation? What if other people in your life became inspired by how you began coping with your challenges?

Twenty years of research, including a major study at the Lombardi Cancer Center at Georgetown University featured in *The Oncologist* and studies by Dr. James Pennebaker, head of the psychology department at the University of Texas, as seen in Harvard Medical School's HEALTH BEAT, reveal that expressive writing—dealing with our deepest thoughts and feelings—can contribute to improved physical and emotional health. For example, patients participating in just one 20-minute writing session reported improvement in their general outlook on cancer and physical quality of life.

Expressive writing can be a therapeutic, educational and artistic tool for anyone coping with chronic illness or life-changing challenges like cancer, divorce, grief or addiction.

Coauthoring Chicken Soup for the Soul's *The Cancer Book* in 2009 confirmed these findings for me. Seeing how 100 different people used writing to cope positively with cancer taught me a great deal about the process and the potential of writing to heal and inspire.

During my subsequent work leading writing workshops in cancer centers around the country, I have seen patients, survivors, caregivers, family, friends and medical staff share a common experience. Expressive writing opens up new doors to deal with a fear of the unknown and the stress of unexpected life changes that come with each and every diagnosis.

But the workshops also challenge participants to reconsider how we communicate by using writing to share our most vulnerable thoughts and feelings.

That's why *Write for Life* exists. It's a place to experiment and play, in spite of the challenges you may be facing. This book may push you out of your comfort zone, scramble things up a bit and help you feel bigger and better. That joy might even spread to those around you. What a gift you could have in store for them!

So that's it in a nutshell. This book offers a helping hand, if only for a moment in your day.

But I also have a personal reason for doing this book. When my dad was diagnosed with acute myeloid leukemia in 1986, I could hardly pronounce it, much less write about it. What was I supposed to write about, anyway? I hardly spoke with my dad's doctors. It just wasn't done back then. My mother couldn't explain much and no one in my family besides my sister really discussed the situation. Denial? Etiquette? A bit of both, I guess. My dad wasn't particularly talkative, anyway, and didn't welcome communication on the subject.

Now, when I see people dealing openly with cancer, I consider them blessed with an ability to communicate and share their feelings, no matter how tough that may be.

This book is meant to honor that and urge others to follow that example. Writing it has required perseverance, as my dad favored, and I thank him for that. If you're wondering about a guide to using this book, see the table of contents and start wherever you like.

KISS. Keep It Simple, Survivor.

Part One

ME:
It's All About Me!

I AM

Fill in the blank:

I AM _____

Human beings naturally fall into obvious categories, with some determined by gender, race, age, religion, profession, political leanings and sexual preference. Some of us place great meaning in those labels, while others put more emphasis on their roles as parents, children, public servants and/or social activists. How society identifies each of us is one thing we must cope with, especially when the labeling becomes "flavored." On the other hand, the way in which we define ourselves carries much more weight.

"Who am I?" touches us on spiritual and pragmatic levels. It can be both an existential and a moment-by-moment question. In times of great change and stress, such as in response to a diagnosis of cancer, our sense of self will be questioned, and the ways in which we previously identified ourselves may be turned upside down. Whether you are a patient or a caregiver of any kind, it's vital that you see life with clear eyes, and that begins each morning when you look in the mirror.

"I AM" can start at your emotional center or it may take off from a more philosophical place. It may incorporate a wide-angle view or focus on the minutie of the moment. There are no rules. But there are compelling reasons for getting in touch with yourself, especially when your very existence is being challenged.

Add three more:

I AM _____

_____

_____

Maybe you identified yourself by gender and/or sexual preference. Did you list physical attributes, religious preference, dietary nature or marital status? What about your parenting philosophy and general outlook on life?

> *I am a stunningly average devilishly handsome male heterosexual Jewish quasi-vegetarian divorced father who loves his kids like crazy doesn't always believe in commas (and lies about his looks).*

But that's just me. How do you label yourself? Maybe you're simply living in the moment and your response to I AM may be nothing more than "Hungry" or "Tired" or "Poor," in which case you qualify for writing a new and famous poem to adorn the Statue of Liberty and you won't be needing this book because you'll be too busy making the rounds of morning talk shows and endorsing small appliances.

But most of us don't live in that rarefied air. Since us normal folks have to figure out we are for ourselves, let's just get to it. After all, part one of this book is all about the proverbial ME.

Why Write About Me?

If you've been diagnosed with cancer, you're probably facing enormous challenges and need to focus a great deal on yourself. If you are a patient's caretaker, doctor or nurse—responsible for someone else's health—you also need to take care of yourself. Writing can help.

That's why this section is devoted to ME: It's All About Me. It's like being a kid again on your birthday. Everything is for me, with me and to me. Me. Me. Me. Celebrate Me. Take care of ME.

Focus on yourself for now. In Part Two, your attention will turn to others as you begin communicating with loved ones, friends and doctors. Eventually, you may wish to share your writing with the general public, inspiring them with your personal perspective on life's priorities.

You may be feeling too raw to imagine that right now. You may simply be intimidated, and the idea of writing rekindles a nightmare called High School English, where your teacher made you write down that yucky stuff called "feelings" in a journal and you forced yourself to produce just enough to secure a passing grade.

Dear Diary: I feel so bad. My teacher is making me express my feelings and all I can feel right now is how much I hate my teacher for making me do this.

Relax. Everyone here passes. Writing is meant to be a tool, not a test. In fact, writing can be just the tool you need right now: 1) for clarifying your thoughts, 2) for relieving stress and 3) for improving communication.

Those are three great reasons to write. I'll take one of each, please. Who can argue with clearing up the haze of a daily overload of information, stimulation and trepidation? Who can object to writing their way to relaxation? Who can rail against the benefits of better communication?

Organization. Relaxation. Communication. Writing can enable all three on a daily basis. But you already knew that! Only thing is, for some reason, you haven't given yourself permission to begin.

"It feels too big."
"Where do I even start?"
"I'm not a writer."

Yeah, yeah, yeah. Are you claiming that in high school you couldn't write your way out of a paper bag, so how can you start now? Or that you've always dreaded sharing your feelings because once you put them down on paper you might have to deal with them? Or do you feel that real men don't write, that they just nod, shrug and change the channel?

In *The Elements of Style,* by William Strunk Jr. and EB White, Rule 17 commands writers to "Omit needless words."

I've already failed miserably. But here's the point. It's your turn to pay attention to you—the big ME—which means digging deep to get in touch with everything you're dealing with: the good, the bad and the ugly. When you do, life becomes more beautiful than it already is.

I AM: Take 2

Pick one of your previous responses and embellish! Don't shy away from details and try to include any trouble spots you might have been ignoring.

I AM _____

TIP
Find a comfortable spot to write and try using pen and paper.

6

Further Ruminations on I AM

In *I AM: The Power of Discovering Who You Really Are* (Tarcher 2010) author Howard Falco says that "The essence of free will is choosing how you will perceive and react to your experience in every moment."

Who do you think you are? Your life may depend on it. Your answers to I AM could go a long way toward defining ME. But that's just for now. ME is fluid, right? One day, you're humming along, texting your friend, when you walk into a street pole and break your nose. Your ME changes. Yesterday, you were amazingly attractive. Today, with that commedia dell'arte mask on your face, bracing your nose against any further damage, your ME is somewhat altered or at least humbled. You're not the same ME as you were pre-collision. Even your mirror will agree. But which ME will you choose to present to the world? It's a question of falling down and getting back up again, as if there's really any other option.

"Fall seven times; stand up eight." This Japanese proverb pretty much sums it up and the best thing about it is—it's short. Fall. Stand. Repeat. Like washing your hair: how hard can it be?

Oh, much more little grasshopper, much more.

Howard Falco, modern-day teacher and speaker on the nature of consciousness, reality and the workings of the mind, offers a clear understanding of the origin of all human action and inaction, joy and suffering, and he honors the experience by sharing what he discovered.

"Fear says, I am not. Faith says, I AM."

He goes on to list how these essential truths are validated.

I AM worthy and have purpose in every moment.
I AM love and I AM loved.
I AM the creator of my experience of life.

Translation: You are the ME you make.

Just like Popeye: "I am what I am."

If a cartoon character could figure it out, so can you. Let's go back to the blanks you filled in on the preceding pages.

What is at the core of what you filled in for I AM? What did you omit? By mistake? By choice? How do you prioritize the process of labeling yourself?

Before you begin any serious ruminating, don't try figuring it out in your head. This is not a multiplication problem. Write down the words—the ones that represent your thoughts and feelings. See them for what they are and who you are. Add to the list if you want. In sum, that you is the ME you are looking for.

Take a moment to look back at what you first wrote.

I AM _____. Keep going.

Sleeping Next to Myself

As my dear friend Dani spiraled deeper and deeper into what turned out to be her last round of cancer treatments, she told me something that made extraordinary sense, because it revealed something central about what happens when trauma causes us to lose a connection to our self.

"Sometimes, I have the feeling I am sleeping next to myself."

Dani said that to me last summer on more than one occasion. She was calm because that was her nature, but she was drifting away from her center, from what had grounded her for such a very long time.

"How do you find yourself again?" I asked her.

"Maybe I don't," she said. "But at least it's me who is looking."

Dani's wisdom and strength revealed something essential in our collective struggle to make sense of our lives, especially in the context of a life stricken by illness. But even as Dani slowed down, grew quieter and began to vanish into her own survival mode, she retained what I could always hear on the phone as her own voice, painfully tired but still clear, even in the confusion and dismay of what was happening to her.

"I can't feel the steps beneath my feet," she said. "I'm floating somewhere, in some place I've never been before. I'm scared, but I have to keep the pilot light going." And so she did for a little while longer.

When I described this book to Dani, she encouraged me to finish it quickly because people who are struggling need to keep looking—for themselves and to others—because that is all we have, when all is said and done.

So, for all of you who may be sleeping next to yourself—or someone you love— this part of the book is for you, as we begin with you—the great ME of your life, the one your life revolves around.

This is the moment to look inside, identify and ultimately share. Feel with your brains. Think from your heart. And like dear Dani, always keep looking.

What Keeps Your Pilot Light Lit?

As all heroes do when facing great odds, they persevere. They summon a magical power to overcome the challenge they are facing, and their triumph inspires us to meet our own trials and tribulations with greater vigor and determination.

We all grew up with numerous fairy tales, featuring princes on white horses, swashbuckling swordsmen slaying dragons and superhuman amazons ridding the earth of evil aliens. But we also see people in our own homes and neighborhoods who are heroes in their own right. Each of us probably has a personal list of men, women and children who have inspired us to live better in some shape or form.

When Dani described how she had to "keep the pilot light going," she got me thinking about my own. What was I doing to keep mine going? What do you do to keep yours lit?

Take a few minutes now to jot down some notes about that. Write directly on this page. That's what it's here for.

Fear: Dumbo is in the House

Since I began teaching writing workshops in cancer centers around the country, I've discovered that, along with the patients, caregivers, survivors, doctors, nurses, researchers, hospital administrators and journalists in attendance, there is also an elephant in every room.

Considering the collective energy of the individual stories gathered together, you could say it's a herd of elephants, floating in our space, waiting to be recognized so they can nod or shrug, while looking a little sheepish, which is a funny image for an airborne elephant.

In the 1941 animated Disney classic *Dumbo,* the star pachyderm faces ridicule because of his unusually large ears. His mother gets locked up for defending her son, and Dumbo is left to grow up without a mother. His only real friend is a mouse who encourages him to use his natural ability to fly. In the end, Dumbo conquers his self-esteem issues and becomes a media sensation. That's my Cliffs Notes version.

Inside the writing workshops, Dumbo is definitely lurking, whether we like it or not. Let's be honest. The elephant in the room in any cancer center is CANCER, itself.

Wait a minute. Am I sure about that? No. I'm not sure because I think the real elephant in the room is FEAR.

If you're a patient who has been diagnosed with cancer, you fear for your own life. If it's a loved one or friend of yours who is facing cancer, you fear for their well-being and survival. If you are a doctor or a nurse, you are facing the same issues, multiplied more than most people could ever imagine.

But the core question for everyone is the same: What are you afraid of? Write it down. Dig deeper. Study it. Pause. Forget. Begin letting go of the fear. Burn the list you just wrote—if you must. Life is too short to be afraid of it, no matter how long it may last.

Face Your Fears

Right here and now, write down your top five fears. Just releasing them from your head onto the page can help a little. Releasing them to a place where you can read them and see them a bit more objectively will help you keep them in their place—to be handled and accepted.

1 _____

2 _____

3 _____

4 _____

5 _____

Blood on the Page

If you feel it, write it. If it hurts, say so. Why hold back? This is your life.

"I'm scared. I feel sick. The chemo made me throw up big, green projectiles of yuk. I'm just cramping up. My stomach feels terrible. It's all terrible. Painful. I was up all night, exhausted; exhausted through the whole night with no sleep. All the next day, I had a hangover from throwing up all night. I didn't have the energy to do it anymore but my body made me heave anyway, over and over again. Could I be vomiting away all the chemo meds? Could this be a total waste? Am I rotting away, in a big, green projectile of my own vomit?"

There. Blood on the page. Cancer in all its glory. No one has to read it. Consider it your own private vomit—unless you need to share; unless that will help ease the burden and give you a head start on moving forward, into the light. Then, by all means, write and share and write some more. Start here.

What hurts?

How do I cope?

Can I get more help?

Who do I want to ask for help?

What words will I use?

The Funny Thing About Cancer Is...

If you could bottle laughter and sell it, pharmacies all over the world would be selling it like hotcakes and turning into palaces. I mean, what feels better than laughing?

For example: Did you hear the one about the doctor who told his patient that he had six months to live? He suggests that he marry a nice Jewish girl and move to a secluded island.

"Will that cure my cancer?" the man asks.

"No," the doctor tells him. "But the six months will go by much slower."

Ba-da-boom!

We've all heard the saying, "Laughter is the best medicine." We've also heard endless claims from shamans, traveling salesmen and websites about holistic, organic cures for everything under the sun. As far as I know, only three things exist that contain the therapeutic qualities needed to cure anything: love, positivity and laughter. Without these three, even the strongest medicine may not do the trick.

When things are bad; when the fear is great and the treatments are harsh; when you're puking all night and your hair falls out; when your wife goes bald or your husband goes limp; when your patients fails or you just don't know what to do, how in God's name are you to survive—even for another day?

Laughter.

We were born with this gift. It can elevate our spirits and make us happy. Laughter is contagious, too. It brings people together. If you get on a good roll, you'll feel stronger and more alive, no matter what shape you're in or how bad you feel.

Norman Cousins, a former editor at the *Saturday Review,* put the concept of laugh therapy on the map in 1976, when his article in the *New England Journal of Medicine* described how he had been afflicted with a rare degenerative disease of the connective tissue. After suffering a series of setbacks in the hospital, he decided to check into a hotel, take massive doses of vitamin C, and watch Marx Brothers movies and read funny books for days on end. Eventually, his symptoms abated and most of the freedom of movement he had lost was regained. Cousins beautifully told his story of the power of the mind on the body in his book, *Anatomy of an Illness* (Norton, 1979). Although no one in the medical community can say for sure what essentially cured Cousins, his story does seem to suggest that love, positivity and laughter can be effective allies in the fight against disease.

First, he loved himself enough to try an alternative means of therapy. Second, he had the positive attitude to stick with it, day after day. Third, he allowed himself an ample enough sense of humor to enjoy himself!

He had fun! So much so, it seems, he wrote an entire book about it.

How Do You Have Fun?

What Makes You Laugh?

Can you list or describe three things that make you laugh? Of course no one will stop you if you keep going, and that is definitely encouraged.

1 _____

2 _____

3 _____

The Healing Power of Laughter

For people living with cancer, it may seem strange or even distasteful to consider humor when facing such serious issues. Yet, laughter can be helpful in ways you might not have realized or imagined. Laughter can help you feel better about yourself and the world around you. Have you looked at the world lately? It's pretty funny. Then again, it's pretty sad, and we need comic relief.

Laughter is a natural diversion. When you laugh, no other thought comes to mind. Laughing can also induce physical changes in the body. After laughing for just a few minutes, you may feel better for hours. When used to supplement conventional cancer treatments, laughter therapy may help in the overall healing process. According to some studies, laughter therapy may provide physical benefits, such as boosting the immune system and circulatory system; enhancing oxygen intake; stimulating the heart and lungs; relaxing muscles throughout the body; triggering the release of endorphins (the body's natural painkillers); easing digestion/soothes stomachaches, relieving pain; balancing blood pressure; and improving mental functions (i.e., alertness, memory, creativity).

Man, this makes me want to stop writing about laughter and look in the mirror—always good for a laugh. Try it. It can't just be my mirror, can it?

Laughter therapy may also improve overall attitude, reduce stress and tension, promote relaxation, aid sleep, enhance quality of life, strengthen social bonds and relationships and produce a general sense of well being.

The Mind-Body Medicine department at Cancer Treatment Centers of America (CTCA) offers supportive alternatives, including laughter therapy, to help patients cope while receiving conventional cancer treatments.

Dr. Katherine Puckett, national director of Mind-Body Medicine at CTCA, first introduced laughter therapy to Midwestern Regional Medical Center upon a patient's request. CTCA now offers humor therapy sessions, also known as Laughter Clubs or humor groups, to help cancer patients and their families use and enjoy laughter as a tool for healing.

Laughter Club is not based on humor or jokes, but on laughter as physical exercise. One exercise involves patients standing in a circle and putting their fingertips on their cheekbones, chest or lower abdomen. They make "ha ha" or "hee hee" sounds until they felt vibrations through their bodies. Dr. Puckett says that during these exercises, it's hard for people not to join in because laughter is so contagious.

According to Dr. Puckett, at the end of a session, patients have said things like "I didn't even think about cancer during Laughter Club" and "That felt great! Things have been so hard that we haven't laughed in months."

An eight-year-old daughter of a CTCA patient who had been struggling with her parent's cancer had a revelation while attending Laughter Club.

"I never thought about laughing everyday, but now I realize I can. Like even when I don't feel happy, I can still laugh and feel better."

Sounds like just what the doctor ordered—or should be.

On the next page, you'll find a prescription for fun and laughter. Enjoy it because you must!

> "The most wasted of all days is one without laughter."
> – E. E. Cummings

Joke Workshop #1

Look at someone sitting near you —in the waiting room of your doctor's office perhaps or on a bus—reading a book or a magazine. Imagine how he or she would sound if they begin to laugh. (Just for fun, imagine everyone in the room or on the bus laughing.) Can you describe all that laughter?

Since laughter is the best medicine—or at least one of them—shouldn't we pay more attention to it where it already exists and try to create it ourselves wherever it's missing? Like right here: I'm just talking about it without writing anything that you could call funny. Except right now.

Poop.

Caught you by surprise, unless you're six.

Poop.

Big fart in a crowded elevator; you're in a business suit, looking serious, and you rip a big, moist one and everybody can't help looking in your direction while you smile a sheepish grin, fart again uncontrollably and say "Whoops!" and laugh, and soon everybody is laughing and the elevator stinks from your badly digested food and stress from life but everyone can relate, 'cause they have issues too, and in no time your gross excuse for good health is bringing everyone together in a lovefest of gas and giggles.

Now, try writing your own funny scene. Right here in the book, on the next page, where it says "My Funny Story." If you'd like, you can steal my fart story to get started.

Stephen King says in *On Writing: A Memoir of the Craft* that "most books about writing are filled with bullshit." Well, who am I to prove him wrong? This book is full of bullshit. Hopefully, it's the fun, constructive kind, like pooping.

My Funny Story

Let's Get Physical

Cambridge International Dictionary of English, whose cover boasts that it "Guides You to the Meaning," was published by Cambridge University Press in 1995, a vintage year for paperback dictionaries. On page 1692, it reads:

writ·ing · *Writing is a person's style of writing with a pen or paper which can be recognized as their own. Writing is also the written work, such as stories or poems, of one person or a group of people. Writing is also the activity of creating pieces of written work, such as stories, poems or articles.*

Writing is a physical thing, so before you do, get comfortable. Find a position where your energy is flowing, not collapsing into a sea of cushions, rendering you mushy brained and sluggish. If you are seeking energy, put yourself in a position to tap what you have. Good posture, active positioning and a slight pitch forward with your body will yield good results.

When you start feeling cramped, get up! Move. Get your blood flowing. Try standing at the kitchen counter and writing. Move around to different places in your house. What about the backyard? The bus stop? Write on a moving bus. Avoid writing under a bus. Most pens—and laptops— are not that durable.

Take your temperature. Sense your mood. If you're feeling dreamy and soft, writing in bed may be a good place. If it's time to be proactive, try sitting at your desk or the dining room table and leaning forward with a positive approach.

Writing does not take place strictly above the ears. The Cambridge International Dictionary refers to a physical malady that too much writing can cause.

Writer's cramp is a painful stiffness in the hand, which people suffer from if they have been writing continuously for a long time.

A simple solution is to write less or buy a dictation device. Really. Talk into a digital recorder and transfer it to your computer. You may find an app on your phone for recording your thoughts and feelings. With notebooks, tablets and voice-activated devices, a world of opportunity exists to express yourself.

Jump!

It's wonderful to slowly learn the process of writing, whether it's journaling, creating essays or scripting a film, to mention just a few possibilities. It's even better when you learn about yourself along the way. I mean, who could argue with a holistic approach to writing?

    A. Republicans
    B. Communists
    C. Hamsters
    D. None of the above

But if you have cancer, love someone who does, or share responsibility for a patient's care, you don't often have the luxury to explore, experiment or embellish. You may need to express yourself right away. How you choose to do it may vary, but it's vital that you jump in and do it. Whether it's through email, texting or the occasional handwritten note sent by carrier pigeon or unsuspecting toddler, if you are connected to a crisis of heath, you will need to share a piece of yourself on a daily basis. If that's a struggle, write stuff down. For example:

Right now, I feel _____

I would feel better if_____

I am afraid of_____

I am worried about _____

I'd like to_____

My To Do List

If you or someone you care about has been diagnosed with cancer, then your "To Do List" has suddenly expanded. That usually includes an entire new set of protocols, from keeping track of doctor's appointments and medication regimens to communicating with family, friends and colleagues about how cancer—directly or indirectly—is affecting your life.

Keeping track of it all can be daunting. Do yourself a favor and get organized. Write down what you need to do and when, who you want to talk to and how you wish to approach them. Each To Do on the list is bound to beg for more. But more is good. It means you're getting things done, including the challenging tasks you may ordinarily avoid.

For instance, you include "Call your brother" on your list. You want to tell him some difficult news. How will he receive it? What words might convey the news best for him? If you prepare by writing down your ideas, it will enable a more productive conversation. Think of it as a rehearsal for the real thing.

There are many reasons for writing down your To Do List. Stating your needs, seeing vital components of your life right there in front of you in black and white, not to mention reminding you to do things you often put off.

Let your list encourage you to live in the moment and guide you with courage into an uncertain future. Take a few minutes to write down the small things, and while you're at it take a stab at the big issues, too. Surprises are waiting with each step you take.

TIP
Leave notebooks around the house and use them!

To Do

Start with some small stuff, for example: Pick up laundry. Buy milk. Feed dog. Take my wife, please.

To Do:

Pick things a bit more demanding, like asking the laundry guy on a date.

To Do:

Select one thing and expand it, like reaching out to your family.

To Do:

Personal Geography

Creating personal narratives can help us process real or imagined experiences and events. By writing down the everyday minutie of our lives, we can piece together a personal history that is reflective in nature and demands us to stay aware of our moment-to-moment existence. This distinguishes fiction from nonfiction, enabling a more clear perception of our place in the world.

Warm Up:

1. List 10 things you do before you get to work or school.

2. List 5 things you see on your way to work or school.

3. List 3 memories from childhood.

4. Explain 1 thing you want to forget.

5. Explain 1 thing you want to always remember.

Details

Details. They poke, pain and please us, from morning through daytime and into the night. Not long ago, 441 days to be exact (detail), I fell in love with a beautiful woman. The minute I saw her I felt a peaceful glow, along with a perfect, pure lust to kiss her—fondly and deep and forever. For the next two and a half hours, I basked in the details of her every gesture and the way she curved her words and crafted pauses. Each time she brushed her thick, black hair away from her angelic face I felt a rush, as if I had just downed a shot of tequila and felt a rush of alcohol infusing my bloodstream. Whenever she grazed a finger along her neck as she laughed, I struggled to keep my smile under wraps, not wanting to appear so obviously slammed. In those spaces between words, I gathered myself, aiming to be almost serious when I spoke, but knowing the only thing serious was how badly I was smitten.

I floated home in a blur, dazzled by the prospect of my life so suddenly transformed. Over the next weeks and months, as we spent more and more time together, I became convinced that I was ready to devote myself to her, one day at a time, for all the days of our lives. But like a reliable soap opera, something changed. She began to withdraw, one gesture at a time, as if she knew I was envisioning the question, the one she could never bring herself to agree with, on principle or just for lack of love, unexplainable, but real. I rolled my eyes, inhaled a breath of deep resignation and turned an old familiar pirouette, letting go in an instant and moving on.

My behavior sounds so healthy, but that's just another illusion. I became a mess—a sad, numb, halfhearted version of the man who had loved large. For weeks, my eyes resembled two sawed-off squirt guns that shot pellets of pain, leaving my face wet and spirit deflated.

But writing saved me. While it exposed the ego-bashing, abject rejection I felt at the time, it also invited me to explore the future with a semblance of hope that I could become whole again.

But enough of my details. It's time for yours.

My Life Story: The Five-Minute Version

Pick any five-minute segment of your life and write about it for five minutes. Include as many details as possible. When you finish, revisit some of what you have previously written in this book, adding new details and nuance.

Life Is Just a Dream — What Are Yours?

My dear friend Bob, may he rest in peace, was something of an honorary Buddhist, and Christian, and Jew—a heathen's heathen according to some but clearly a spiritual man to those who knew him.

"David, it's all just a dream," he told me once.

While I have a fondness for phrases like that and appreciate their charm, the way Bob said it—with such joy and sincerity—was totally convincing, as if he was telling me from actual experience. I believed him then and still do now.

"It's all just a dream."

So, what does that mean? While it resonates differently for each of us, it still must be about softening our heart, accepting what is in front of us and living with joy in the moment. I mean, what other choice do we have?

Okay. You may say, "I have cancer. That's no dream."

Or "Getting divorced really sucks. What's the dream in that?"

"My only child is gone to college—and essentially gone forever from my life. I'm not dreaming! He's gone!"

We live minute to minute, hour by hour, and one day at a time. Venturing further than that is a stretch, as we can only exist (and be awake) in the moment we are living. But some people—long-range planners—are particularly good at thinking ahead, and when they do, it's often because they write stuff down!

I'm saying things that may contradict each other. First, I'm questioning the idea of planning ahead if it means living less in the moment. At the same time, I admire people who plan for their future. But are they missing something now while they concentrate on what doesn't yet exist? When you throw in the past as a contextual frame, we are living in three tenses at once. Our high school English teachers would frown upon that if we did so in an essay assignment, but in real life we do it all the time. So, now that I've mused on that, I surrender my argument.

Be here now, with a nod to the past and an eye on the future. But no matter which way you lean at any moment—write stuff down! Unless you have an Einstein-like ability to keep everything fresh in your mind, ready to share at any moment, you will forget most of what you think about. Guaranteed! So write it down right away and consider its relative value later.

Back to our theme—Life is just a dream. So what are yours? If I may indulge you, write them down, one at a time—the big ones, the dreams that keep you up at night and the little ones that nibble at you during the day, forgotten by the time you get home. Keep track of the silly ones, those that require violin accompaniment and the ones that end in bloodshed. Record them, one dream a day. After a month, revisit your list. By then, you'll already have new ones.

I believe we are always dreaming; it's just that we are asleep much of the time and not paying attention. Or we are too busy, way too busy, to hear the music in our minds and the wistful wanderings of our hearts.

Slow down. Listen to yourself. Some things may be way out of tune. (I'm killing this musical metaphor, huh?) When you write, you re-align yourself; you get back on track, which means being at one with your breath—in sync—when the energy of life, inside and out, is in your control. That is when writing much more than useful; it becomes exciting.

What Are Your Dreams?

What is the perfect time to document a dream? How about now?

Journey to Nowhere

If you know the song "Road to Nowhere" by the Talking Heads, may I suggest you hum it softly while reading this.

Did you ever just get in your car and go for an aimless drive? It may have been a long time ago, before gas prices went crazy, but do you remember what that felt like? Wasn't it cool to get behind the wheel and take off, with no particular destination in mind? Ever hop on a subway with the same idea? Just ride and ride until BAM! You hop off at a stop you've never been to before. The extravagant version of this kind of spontaneity would be going to the airport and taking the first flight out to a city that would suddenly become your city of choice.

"Baby, it's all right, baby it's all right…"

When it comes to writing, there's a parallel universe worth exploring. In the first scenario, you grab a "writing device" and start writing, with no particular destination in mind, satisfying an urge to express yourself.

"When I woke up this morning, I felt good."

Perhaps you feel the need to analyze your feelings.

"That surprised me because I didn't sleep well. I wonder why. Maybe it's because I'm feeling anxious about something."

In the second scene, you eventually get off the subway at an unfamiliar station and embark on a new adventure.

"I need to identify what's making me lose sleep at night. Maybe if I make a list of what troubles me I can figure it out."

Finally, you take a real plunge by going to the airport and doing something TEACHER totally out-of-the-box.

"I haven't written a poem since I was a lovesick teenager but here goes…"

Your journey to nowhere is just a journey into the unknown. We face that each day, to varying degrees. If you've been diagnosed with cancer, sued for divorce or fired from your job, you are probably beginning a similar trip into the unknown. Don't go it alone.

Travel Games & Mental Engineering Exercises

Every writer must cultivate a sense of specifics, from observing the environment to the sound of one's voice and the exact clothing one is wearing. Focusing on details has other advantages, too, like preparing questions and describing symptoms for an upcoming doctor's appointment. If you write everything down, you won't forget half of what you wanted to ask or discuss.

Flash Rosenberg inspired these games and exercises[1] from an adult education class she invented at the Cooper Union in New York City, titled Underground Creativity: Subway Games and Inquiries. Flash intended to sharpen her students' sense of observation and humor by having them express what it's like to be immersed in a crowd with their own thoughts.

"Personally," she says, "I have always found the lilt and dash of commuting to be such an inspired time to think."

While Flash's Subway Games are meant to deepen skills in writing, drawing and photography, let's focus on what writing offers, whether you're traveling on a subway, train or bus. Here are a few questions to get you started.

What did you notice first about the person sitting across from you?

What did this person have for breakfast, lunch or dinner?

Would I wear any of the clothes that this person has on?

Why do you imagine this person is riding the bus?

---

[1] FLASH ROSENBERG is a photographer, writer, performer, filmmaker and cartoonist based in New York City. She is artist-in-residence at the New York City Public Library and a 2011 Guggenheim Fellow. Her favorite answer is "Okay!"

Where do you think he or she may be going?

What will people think when they see you feverishly scribbling?

What you notice about someone else says much about you. The point of the exercise is not just to see if you can write on a moving vehicle; it's to open your mind to see the world you are living in.

COUNT!

As you board the vehicle you're traveling in, start counting. It will help you pay attention to your environment, be specific and focus. For example, how many:

seats:	_____	people:	_____
windows:	_____	bags:	_____
languages:	_____	moods:	_____
hats:	_____	children:	_____

How many more things can you count?

SHOE / FACE

Look at the shoes of someone sitting near you. Guess how his or her face might look. Describe it with words or by drawing.

This game asks you to link real evidence with imagined associations, which demonstrates how we make assumptions, interpret impressions and manage expectations. Understanding that may educate us about how we judge people and communicate with them. It may also help us develop story lines and characters.

GIVE UP YOUR SEAT

As soon as someone gets on the bus or comes down the aisle of your train, get up and give them your seat. Why? It's cool to be kind, their reaction may be nice and you may meet the person of your dreams. Even better, giving away your seat to someone who needs it more will help you feel a little stronger. Even while standing for the duration of your trip, jot down a few notes about the experience.

Note: If you are tired or feeling low, save this game for a better day.

HATE THAT!

This is great to play when you're having a bad day because it ultimately makes light of your biggest annoyances. Make a list of everything that bugs you. For example: People who sit with their legs spread wide and hog up three seats OR someone speaking loudly on a cell phone OR the car, bus or train you're riding hitting the brakes too often and too hard. As soon as you identify a pet peeve, write it down and cross it out with the words *Hate That!*

There are much nastier versions of this game. I could suggest one, but then I'd be reliving a painful part of my life and facing the threat of legal action. Let's just say I would definitely *Hate That!*

WHAT'S IN THE BAG?

Study a person's bag or backpack. What do you think is in there? The contents of a woman's purse speak volumes about the size of her…purse. Seriously, as many actors do when inhabiting a role, examining the details of a person's life can be quite revealing. You may find a complete memoir in someone's handbag, a soap opera bouncing inside a backpack and a cesspool of truth in more briefcases than you could imagine. All are fertile ground for writing!

MAKE A WISH

Pick three strangers riding with you and write what you think each of them might secretly be wishing for at that very minute.

Abandoning the But

Why do we put stuff off until tomorrow—or next week or next year? It can't just be laziness. We all drink too much coffee for that. There must be other reasons—and a bevy of excuses.

> *"But it can wait."*
> *"But it's too hard."*
> *"I'm just not ready. But when I feel more confident, I'll go for it."*

Overcoming procrastination, conquering fears and a addressing a complicated web of self-esteem issues can keep us from moving forward. When any or all of these thoughts start swimming around in our heads, it's easy to feel overwhelmed and become paralyzed. As a result, we may remain stuck where we don't belong or have any need to be.

The act of writing—expressing our deepest thoughts and fears and our greatest joys and loves—can set us free and make our lives bigger and better. Instead of going numb in front of the television or disappearing at the mall, we can choose to abandon the "buts" by facing our worries, challenging our apprehensions and embracing our foibles.

Imagine jumping into a lake, maybe even a cold one up in the mountains. You may seriously hesitate, and after wagging a toe in the water you may back off, waiting for someone else to take the first plunge. You close your eyes and wonder if this could be your moment. And then something makes you jump!

As you penetrate the water, it's a perfect, shocking moment that wakes you up, making you come alive in a way that few other activities can rival. This is often followed by a chain reaction of exhilaration, satisfaction and joy.

Seize the moment. Grab a notebook or keyboard. Take the plunge.

The Cheapest Therapist in Town

When I was growing up in New England, I didn't meet a single soul who saw a shrink. I never saw a therapist's shingle advertising its presence or services. Does that mean everyone in town was self-sustaining? Really? Hard to imagine, especially in this day and age of what seems like therapists on every block—for ladies and gentlemen, children of all ages, and the rest of you. And let's not forget your pets. They have feelings, too.

Point of confession: I have benefited from a few sessions here and there. A loaded divorce will do that to you. But for most of my life, I have sought the help of the same therapeutic aide. These eyes and ears can accompany me anywhere, anytime, and have become a friend and confidant.

My hopes, my dreams, my humiliations and my mistakes—all included for the same price. There's no time limit, either, and I can express myself in whatever fashion I want—sweet, nasty, naughty or nice. I can be deep one minute and alarmingly superficial the next. The best thing is, I am never judged or corrected.

I can monitor my own bad behavior and encourage myself to continue on whatever good pathways I have developed. It's all good. Even better, everything I talk about is recorded so I can always refer back to whatever I need. And best of all, for decades it's been almost free.

The first notebook I bought at Woolworth's cost less than a lollipop, and the multipurpose mixed media personal journal I purchased online last week, complete with my name monogrammed on the cover with a pocket for my phone, a headphone jack to listen to my tunes, a Swiss Army knife and a miniature umbrella—cost about the same as one movie admission. That's a bargain because I can watch a flick for two hours but I can write in that journal and plug into my business for weeks and months. Okay, I'm kidding about the multipurpose mixed media personal journal, but a notebook costs essentially nothing and its therapeutic effects are well documented.

Morning Notes

In *The Artist's Way,* Julia Cameron talks about the benefits of getting up each day and immediately writing your own version of "morning pages," the stuff that spills out of your mind before you've even washed your face. She recommends three pages, which is really ambitious (woops, speaking for myself), but why not? It could be quite refreshing to see what you come up with before you've really woken up.

While my personal goal is the great American novel, a more reasonable expectation might be half a page of fragmented notes. Between daily deadlines, family obligations and a plethora of welcome and thoroughly distasteful distractions, I think I can be relatively happy with something in between.

I'll call it *The Pretty Good American Book That Might Make the World a Better Place for Some People Even in a Small Way And That's Worthwhile Too.*

Oh wait, that's this book. I did it.

I don't wake up each morning and write pages. If only. Sometimes I do, and it's liberating. It feels as if I have original thoughts of my own, before the emerging day—and the rest of the world—corrupt my virginal mind. If only. But seriously, it's something like that. First thing in the morning, before the engines are up to full speed, remarkable little revelations may pop out of your pen.

I often enjoy rambling forays at my computer in the middle of the night, blasting through the gaps in my brain by pounding relentlessly on the keyboard, hoping that something will stick and pass muster in the light of a new day. That's when I am my own harshest critic but also indulgent, especially when I think I might be able to help someone.

Remember that cheap notebook on the preceding page? Or whatever electronic device you favor? Both are so easy and available. Now, it's simply a matter of figuring out why you need to use them!

Why We Write

Expressive writing can be much more useful than merely recording your private thoughts and feelings in a journal or diary. Clearing your mind, opening your heart and elevating your soul are absolutely important, but what is any of that worth if it doesn't lead you to becoming a better communicator? Ultimately, we're here on earth to live and learn and love in the company of others. As far as I know. This requires effective communication. Basic stuff. Common sense. Let's start there. That is why we write. But there's more.

Mindy Greenstein, PhD[2], clinical psychologist, psycho-oncologist and author of *The House on Crash Corner,* a bold and startling collection of essays, has a lot to say about why we write. In her blog, *The Flip Side,* Mindy discusses the value of storytelling and the need for meaning. Even more important, she reveals the value of humor.

What do books do for us, exactly? For one thing, they teach. Teach us how to do specific things—whether it's the book that taught my son Isaac how to strengthen his pitching arm, or the ones I consulted when trying to design a website. They also divert and amuse. In Getting Even, *Woody Allen didn't teach me anything I deemed worth knowing about the world. But my laughter was justification enough for its existence. The best books often do both—teach and amuse at the same time. Joseph Heller's* Catch-22 *has a lot to teach about the hell of war, but he does it in the context of having first made us laugh.*

There's also a third use of books, but humor is too important not to explore more fully first. My favorite definition comes from Mel Brooks's 2,000-year-old man, whose description recalls Sigmund Freud's.

"Tragedy is if I'll cut my finger, that's tragedy. It bleeds, and I'll cry and I'll run around and go to Mount Sinai for a day and a

---

[2] Former Chief Clinical Fellow in the Department of Psychiatry and Behavioral Sciences at Memorial Sloan Kettering Cancer Center, where she also co-developed the Meaning-Centered Group Psychotherapy intervention. Please visit www.mindygreenstein.com.

half. I'm very nervous about it. And to me, comedy is if you walk into an open sewer and die. What do I care?"

Hence, the saying, "Comedy is tragedy that happens to somebody else." The first known comedian, according to Brooks, is Murray the Nut, who gives his cavemates their first taste of laughter when he gets himself eaten by a lion.

To give you a sense of just how important humor is—even Viktor Frankl, the famous Viennese psychiatrist who wrote Man's Search for Meaning, *once gave someone a therapeutic homework assignment to tell a funny story every day—and that was in Auschwitz, where he and his "patient" were inmates at the time. The men in the concentration camp barracks spontaneously put together a cabaret show by moving benches around and starting to sing or clown around and tell stories. As soon as other inmates heard about it, they poured into the room as if it were opening night at the Copacabana. Some of them even missed their daily rations of food, which were being distributed at the same time, because they considered the gathering too much nourishment for their souls to pass up.*

Frankl regarded humor as a device for distancing yourself from your misery. Perhaps the 2,000-year-old man's definition helps us see how. Humor creates a perspective change—literally—as if the sufferer is now some other poor schnook he's watching, rather than himself. Seeing the story from a distance makes it easier to see the humor and finding it funny makes it easier to create that distance. For the same reason I've gotten some of my funniest stories from my experiences as a cancer patient.

This excerpt from Mindy's 2012 blog, included here with her kind permission, demonstrates the enduring beauty of humor and the need for personal expression in the midst of traumatic, life-threatening circumstances. Mindy's keen eye and deft touch seem a fitting conclusion to Part One and a perfect link to Part Two. Thank you Mindy. Enjoy!

Before moving on, please take a moment to consider why you write.

Why I Write

I write because _____

I write whenever I feel _____

Writing helps me with _____

I wish I could write about _____

Writing will open up doors to _____

I think I could write more if I _____

TIP
Leave notebooks around the house and use them!

PART TWO

YOU:
It's All About You!
(and Me)

From Me to You

In Part One, we took the necessary "ME" approach, a self-centered look at what each of us need in times of crisis, whether we are a patient, survivor, caregiver or anyone affected by a cancer diagnosis.

In Part Two, let's consider the "YOU" factor— what it means to express yourself and connect with others, be it your spouse, child, neighbor, clergy or doctor. Cancer can inspire you to appreciate your life—that same one you've taken for granted for so long. You may rekindle closeness with your spouse you haven't experienced in years. Cancer may lead you to mend a family relationship, seek counsel from a new source or communicate with your doctor on an unexpected level.

Don't worry. There's still ample opportunity to be selfish and pamper yourself. But that can grow tiresome. No man is an island, etc., except those living peacefully on an actual island, and I can only hope this book reaches them, especially if that means I deliver it personally. But for now, from me to you, let's get busy.

Join the Club

The moment you get diagnosed with cancer you suddenly become a member of an unofficial but amazing club, albeit one you never had any intention of joining. Of course you don't want to be a permanent member, if there is any such thing. Instead, you want to join a different club as soon as possible— the survivors club, for example, and become a permanent member of that. Then again, since we're not dealing with any real permanence—cancer or not—perhaps we shouldn't go out and get those cards laminated.

I'm not recommending that anyone identify himself on a daily basis by their cancer, but it's guaranteed that there will be times when that is your predominant means of identification. In those moments, I suggest that you surrender. Why not join the club? Why not seek the support of a group greater than yourself? Why not share your singular experience?

When I am forced to wait in line at a post office (how quaint) or in an unemployment line (how sad), I like to meet other people sharing the same predicament. We are a motley crew that would rather be somewhere else. But in that moment—correction—in those long, long, seemingly forever moments of coping with frustration and fury, we have something in common. We are a community.

Honestly, I have met some wonderful people while waiting in line. Some of us still gather on a monthly basis, to stand together and fidget, to pace, to complain and to celebrate our common connection.

So here is your opportunity to join the club. It may be The Patient Club, The Survivor Club, The Caretaker Club or The Concerned Friend Club. Whichever it is, you have a chance to make the most of it. It's an invitation to secure real relationships with real people sharing real stories.

Club Application

Name _____

Club Affiliation _____

Reason for Joining Club _____

Expectations_____

Apprehensions _____

Strengths_____

Weaknesses_____

Suggestions_____

The Benefits of Gratitude

We all know that a simple "thank you" can go a long way. But gratitude means much more than simple good behavior. No matter how bad life gets, there is usually something to be grateful for. If we "look harder," as Rafiki suggests in *The Lion King*[3] we will notice there is plenty to acknowledge.

Annette Ramke and Kendall Scott, the authors of *Kicking Cancer in the Kitchen: The Girlfriend's Cookbook and Guide to Using Real Food to Fight Cancer* (Running Press, 2012), have good advice when it comes to capitalizing on gratitude.

"Try our favorite tip and grab yourself a gratitude journal. Pick a pretty one you will enjoy using and place it in a spot where you will see it every day—near your bed or on your desk, for example. Then take a few minutes daily to write down at least ten things you are thankful for."

Personally, I wouldn't use the word "pretty" to describe my journals. But that's just me, hung up on my brutally masculine self-image. I prefer the smoldering, refined and introspective look of black leather—or a pastel legal pad. Whatever. Just write. If you can't find ten things you're thankful for, repeat the ones worth repeating. You can never be too thankful, right?

When life delivers a curveball, we are forced to reevaluate our priorities. But no matter how we reshuffle things, it's usually clear who the people are that matter most and the things that carry the greatest meaning in our lives. For all of that, we are grateful, even if we don't always recognize or show it.

Start with the people in your life who care about you. Then, consider the doctors, nurses, lab technicians, etc., who have taken care of you or are responsible for your loved one, friend or foe. Express yourself to them.

That's what this part is all about: communicating! By answering a few questions on the next page, you'll be on your way.

---

[3] My son's favorite movie as a child. We watched it together an estimated 73 times.

Gratitude 101

What are you grateful for? List five things.

How can you take more time in your life to connect with them?

Who are your grateful for? List five people.

Is it time to acknowledge them? Why not begin right now?

What lessons are you currently learning that you are grateful for?

How can you recognize the people responsible for them?

Help!

You're hurting. Tired. Scared. Overwhelmed. Your spouse is, too. But you need to discuss your feelings, and that requires a willing, listening partner. Where to start? It feels so big. How do I speak my peace and not burden the one I love?

Organizing those emotions on paper will help you harness such big feelings. When you look at your words on the page and say them out loud you will own your thoughts and feelings, making them much easier to share with your family, friends and doctors. At this point, writing is not about getting published or winning prizes. It's about self-expression and feeling better.

Let's reconsider what it means involved to ask for help. Our egos are on the line. No one wants to feel needy, no matter what the reason may be. And if you're the caretaker, it can be like walking on eggshells. You want to get it right. You want to help. I mean, damn! The person you love needs you! But you don't want to hover, making that person feel needy. It's hard to find the right balance.

In times of great stress, we get stuck in our own heads, nearly frozen with anxiety. We have to find a way to awaken ourselves and live through each moment. Writing down our thoughts and feelings empowers us to own them and consequently to communicate more clearly. You owe this to yourself and the people you care for most.

My Wish List

I wish I could communicate better with _____

Because _____

I wish I could tell him/her that _____

I wish they would help me _____

I like it when they help me because _____

I wish they would not _____

I also wish I could communicate more with _____

I wish I knew how to _____

I wish I could ask for _____

How Do I Tell People?

It's Monday morning, and after an amazing weekend you run into your good friend in the employee lounge.

"How was your weekend?" she asks. Wink wink. As if she knows just by looking at your flushed, hung-over face that your whole world was rocked to the max over the last 48 hours.

"Oh my God, it was amaaaazing!" you reply. "Epic, just epic."

Hmm. Nice. Like that first time you rode a bike or kissed someone for real. Those moments leave us with indelible memories. It feels like we will remember them forever, along with where we were on 9–11 or how time stood still in exquisite perfection when our children were born.

If only we could be playwrights and screenwriters at those times, equipped with the ability to capture these wondrous moments on paper—for prosperity. Some of us try. We write poems and letters and emails and texts, trying to capture what it felt like to be moved so intensely, and to share how seriously jazzed we've been by our very own life.

But what happens when the news is not so rosy? What do we say when we have to tell a different sort of truth, one loaded with trepidation and ripe with a fear of the unknown? If this sounds like a cancer diagnosis, it certainly could be. What do you do when that happens? How do you share that news with your family and friends?

There's no way to prepare for that moment. Impossible. But you can learn from others who have faced this head-on. You breathe deep; you actually practice out loud; yes, you say the words out loud, the words *you* choose to use. Maybe you write them down first, because the very act of doing so gives you a needed sense of control. Write down the words and make them yours. This will help you share them with others.

One-Minute Play

Telling your loved one you have cancer (or telling a patient they do) may be unprecedented, but it can be rehearsed.

Cast yourself as the central character in this one-minute play, with

_____

(fill in the blank with the name of your spouse or best friend), as your co-star, later to be nominated as "Best Supporting Actor."

Title of Play:

_____

Setting:

_____

Time:

_____

Main Objective:

_____

Elizabeth Bayer on "Languaging"

Included in the pages of Chicken Soup for the Soul's *The Cancer Book* is an inspirational memoir by Elizabeth Bayer called *It's Just a Word: Reclaiming Your Life Through Cancer—BEAUTIFULLY.* It was written to help patients and doctors view cancer in a different light.

"The book is about how one can choose to accept a cancer diagnosis," said Elizabeth, "and move through all that it brings with gratitude and love."

Elizabeth was especially concerned about how newly diagnosed patients speak to their families, caretakers and doctors. She was obsessed about the specific language to be used because she considered the choice of words to be indicative of the patient's mind-set and ultimately, their physical, psychological and emotional wellbeing.

When Elizabeth was first diagnosed with cancer, she made a crucial distinction between what she told herself and what her doctor told her. She was determined to create a story that made sense for *her* life, and as her story changed, so did she. Instead of immediately downloading a laundry list of fearful images that would negatively impact her energy field, Elizabeth chose to "language" the news by saying, "I have been diagnosed with cancer," rather than "I have cancer." She found that saying it the first way gave her a degree of separation and detachment that was both empowering and liberating.

Elizabeth was not in denial. She merely chose not to carry anyone's baggage about the word, including her own. That enabled her to move through her subsequent dialogues with doctors and menu of treatments in a gentler and more positive manner.

Instead of cancer happening TO Elizabeth, she saw cancer happening FOR her. This not only benefited Elizabeth. It was instructive for her doctors. Becky Natrajan, MD, PC, Elizabeth's gastroenterologist, said "Elizabeth's wisdom, humility and loving-kindness not only had a great bearing on her own survival; they altered my approach to treating her and future patients—before and after surgery, and throughout their entire recovery period."

Your Personal Language

What words would you choose to share difficult news? How would you begin, especially with a spouse or with children? Will your choice of words make a difference for you?

Try writing a few options—right here. Read them over, perhaps out loud, and see what feels best. Practice saying the words you choose. That will help you feel more confident when you share them. Your loved ones will feel better that way, too, as they digest the news.

Taking Care of Our Doctors

Any parent will tell you that being taken for granted comes with the territory. From worrying about babies and toddlers 24/7 to being raked over the coals by a rude and nasty teen, parents consistently deal with exhaustion, guilt, and feelings of complete inadequacy. Not that I ever experienced those feelings with my kids. (Hold on please, while I remove tongue from cheek.)

This parental merry-go-round could be mistaken for a doctor's daily diet of challenges, sans the fatal possibilities. But to be fair, what happens to the doctor who deals with cancer patients—and death—every freaking day? Unlike parents who at least have Mothers Day and Fathers Day, who is looking out for doctors? Do we have any idea what the average oncology doctor and nurse go through each and every day?

Do Doctors Grieve?

According to Leeat Granek, a health psychologist and postdoctoral fellow at the Hospital for Sick Children in Toronto, Canada, grief is seldom discussed within the medical profession—at least not openly. But, as Granek wrote in the *New York Times* on May 27, 2012, "Not only do doctors experience grief, but the professional taboo on the emotion also has negative consequences for the doctors themselves, as well as for the quality of care they provide." These findings are a result of research published in the Archives of Internal Medicine.[4]

How Do Doctors and Nurses Cope?

The oncologists interviewed said that they struggled to "manage their feelings of grief with the detachment they felt was necessary to do their job." Feelings of failure, self-doubt, sadness and powerlessness were not unusual, and a third talked about feelings of guilt, loss of sleep and crying.

The study showed that "grief in the medical context is considered shameful and unprofessional. Even though participants wrestled with feelings of grief, they hid them from others because

---

[4] http://archinte.jamanetwork.com/article.aspx?articleid=1160665

showing emotion was considered a sign of weakness. In fact, many remarked that our interview was the first time they had been asked these questions or spoken about these emotions at all."

The cumulative effects of dealing with these emotions can be daunting. Unsurprisingly, doctors often experience side effects such as inattentiveness, impatience, irritability, emotional exhaustion and burnout. Sound familiar? Any of these issues can negatively impact an oncologist's personal life, too, which may compromise the doctor–patient reltionship.

What Are the Consequences for Patients and their Loved Ones?

According to Granek, research demonstrates that "Unease with losing patients also affected the doctors' ability to communicate about end-of-life issues with patients and their families. Half of our participants said they distanced themselves and withdrew as the patients got closer to dying. This meant fewer visits in the hospital, fewer bedside visits and less overall effort directed toward the dying patient."

Sounds bad for patients and their families. It's quite under-standable that many physicians, especially those dealing with terminal illness and end-of-life issues, must create emotional "safe zones" where they can survive the daily rigors of treating dying patients and their loved ones. No one wants to see a doctor or nurse breaking down on the job. But at what price do medical professionals keep it together?

How Can Doctors Handle the Overwhelming Stress?

Oncologists—and many other medical professionals—do not receive specific training to cope with their own grief or that of their patients and their families. This needs to change, beginning with premed education and continuing right through residency programs as new doctors come into more contact with real patients. As death is part of life, it must be acknowledged and communicated, especially in medical settings.

Dr. Granek writes that, "To improve the quality of end-of-life care for patients and their families, we also need to improve the quality of life of their physicians, making space for them to grieve like everyone else."

In times of great vulnerability, patients and their loved ones need more than a great medical doctor. They need an authentic, sensitive and effective communicator. Really! It's not enough to prescribe the right pills. Sick people need to be cared for—heart and soul.

But here is the problem. Most doctors do not have the training. They practice medicine but they don't practice communication. They can write charts but can't chart their own feelings. They are good at listening to your lungs but not so good at paying attention to your fears.

We Can Help

Dr. Stephen Malamud, an oncologist at Beth Israel Medical Center in New York City and associate professor of clinical medicine at Albert Einstein College of Medicine, supports the value of expressive writing as a supplemental therapy for those diagnosed with cancer. He cites anecdotal evidence from his patients, how they benefit from expressing themselves to him through writing emails as well as preparing for visits by writing notes and keeping journals. Equally important, he reports that communicating by email with his patients has significantly helped him, too.

That leads me to believe that expressive writing—even ten to twenty minutes a day—could be an enormous help for doctors and nurses, especially those dealing with the demands of treating cancer.

Medicine must be more than a one-way street. When patients gently demand better communication with their doctors they will not only be helping themselves. They will be leading their caretakers down a broader, more benevolent road of humanity.

Dear Doctor: A Writing Project

I would like to thank Harriet Berman, PhD and Claire Willis, LICSW, for generously sharing the work they are doing in Massachusetts to foster better relations between patients and doctors. Their efforts to create empathic relationships between these two parties involved patients writing unsent letters to their doctors.

They asked participants to choose an issue they wanted to communicate with their doctor but had not yet managed to do. Suggested topics included:

- How information has been delivered
- How exchanges of information have occurred
- Personal anecdotes
- Your response to information your doctor has shared with you
- Satisfying conversations you have had with your doctor
- Frustrations you have experienced in the course of your care
- Expressions of gratitude
- Expressions of grief, sadness and/or loss
- Things you wish your doctor knew about you
- Things you wish you knew about your doctor
- Questions that you have not yet asked

It was suggested that the letter should be no more than 500 words or two pages. Their group reviewed the letters with an eye toward exploring more deeply some of the issues, thoughts and feelings that too often go unspoken between patient and doctor. Through letter writing, it is hoped that patients will find the words to express themselves with clarity and increase their confidence to speak with their doctors openly and honestly.

Since this book is all about self-expression and improving communication, it seems apropos to take the inspiring work of Harriet Berman, PhD and Claire Willis, LICSW and run with it.

Dear Doctor

TIP
Keep it short. Doctors are busy, but don't
shortchange yourself.

56

An Ode to Caregivers

Psychiatrist Mark Banschick, MD, with whom I coauthored *The Intelligent Divorce*, writes a monthly column for PsychologyToday. com. The following (abbreviated) story appeared in his March 7, 2013 column:

"You're a Caregiver, You're a Hero, and You're Exhausted"

Case Example: Jody's husband, Sam was just diagnosed with a treatable form of cancer. Everything has changed. Sam had always been full of energy, the center of the party. Now, he's tired all the time and comes home from work exhausted and ready for bed. Their four children continue to live their lives, but Jody is constantly on the lookout for problems. Is Harry, their teenage boy getting his work done? Will her two middle children break down? And, what does Jody say to her eight-year-old daughter, Caroline, who constantly asks, "How do you know that Daddy is going to be okay?" It is too much.

But, Jody has a life to live. Sam gets his chemotherapy. Jody takes time off from work to join him. Sam is moody and needy but can't help it. Jody wants to set limits but can't. He asks and she supplies. The give and take is almost gone. Jody fluctuates between exhaustion, anger, loneliness and determination. She cannot put her needs first. Too much is at stake.

No one asks to be a caregiver: *At first, Jody gives up her own needs by necessity. How can she take the time for exercise or friends when Sam is so needy (with good reason), the kids require a functioning parent and Jody still has to work? The gym goes, dates with friends go and religious events go as well. Jody becomes protective of her time and rest. Only the necessities remain.*

Is Jody depressed? No, she is oppressed. Life has thrown her a handful. Jody's in the full swing of life—marriage, kids, work—and now everything has changed. The question is how to best deal with this.

The caregiver is heroic: *It's time to step out of your needs to take care of someone you love. It's that simple and that hard. But just because someone you love is in trouble doesn't mean your needs just go away. Assuming the caregiver role includes building a bridge back to yourself.*

Dr. Banschick goes on to discuss the critical importance of acceptance, being kind to yourself and seeking professional help, either in a support group or with a therapist. He also mentions the healing benefits of sleep, securing a support system, and spirituality. There is much to be learned from his advice.

If you were Jody, I'd suggest you write a letter to Sam, describing what it's like to be in your position, what you feel, what you're afraid of, what you cherish, all those things you may not take the time—or have the courage—to say in person. But you can try explaining yourself on paper—or your laptop. Maybe you'll share it with Sam; maybe you won't.

And if you're Sam, take a moment to consider Jody and all that she's going through, trying to take care of you, your kids and your household, going to work, doctor's appointments and treatments, and all the while living with unprecedented anxiousness—about you, herself and your family. Like Jody, you can try explaining yourself on paper—or your laptop. Maybe you'll share it with her; maybe you won't.

This suggests an intimate pen pal festival. Imagine—spouses really expressing themselves to each other! Parents and children exposing their feelings! This could be the start of something big.

A Personal Warm Up

Before you jump into that cold lake and actually start spilling your guts out to your spouse, child or secret Santa, here are a few helpful prompts to warm you up.

I love you like_____

Without you I _____

Please remember I am _____

It feels great with you when _____

You make me feel bad when _____

I wish we could _____

The Letter I've Been Waiting to Write

Dear Jody or Sam or_____

Joke Workshop #2

Since we've just discussed relationship dynamics, is there a better time to reexplore humor? With men and women, the joke is obvious. From head to toe, we are different. The biggest distinction may be between our ears, where, according to scientists, the disparity between men and women is greatest. Specifically, this means the corpus callosum, the area of our brain operating as the central station for connecting our left and right hemispheres. In women, this valuable piece of real estate is proportionately larger than in men, which explains in a nutshell why most women are capable of articulate expression while men lag behind somewhat in this area.

Looking closer at the science of it all, it's not even fair. In the Olympics of Communication, men face an almost insurmountable disadvantage. In fact, it's a wonder so many men have overcome this distinct handicap. Some would argue that most haven't. Those would probably be women, and there's a good chance that many of them are married to a handicapped man.

Dave Ames, author of *Me, My Cells, and I: A Survivor's Seriously Funny Guide to the Science of Cancer* (Sentient Publications 2011) explains it well.

"By the time a man figures out what to say it's generally not his turn to talk anymore. The woman is way ahead of him, since the female brain has emotional centers in both hemispheres of the brain, enabling more direct access to her feelings and the feelings of others as she puts her emotions into words. Talking between sexes just isn't a fair contest."

True enough, and many would claim that increased access to one's feelings could compound any conflict. Those would probably be men, opining about their wives—that is, until they walk into the room.

In any case, this calls for a joke, but one you create yourself, based upon this comedy of errors we call relationships. See if you can communicate with your spouse (or equivalent) in a manner that aims to balance the inequity in what nature has provided. The attempt alone should be worth a good laugh.

The Value of Music

We've all grown up with a soundtrack to our lives, with a story accompanying each song we remember. List five songs and a memory each one triggers. You'll eventually create a personal story album, inspired by the songs you love most.

1. _____

Memory: _____

2. _____

Memory: _____

3. _____

Memory: _____

4. _____

Memory: _____

5. _____

Memory: _____

A Gift of Music

If you or someone you know will be hospitalized or spending endless hours on a chemo drip, consider creating a personalized iPod full of favorite music. Music can ease pain, induce sleep and stimulate healing.

Active Listening

In an age of relentless online communication, person-to-person listening skills are often underestimated and overlooked. But in a moment of crisis, listening—really paying attention—is crucially important. It's the key to effective communication and writing is an essential tool for making it happen.

It's a team effort. One party talks while the other listens. Then they switch. If there is a modicum of trust and mutual respect, speaking and listening establish what we affectionately call effective communication. Any halfway mature adult[5] can accomplish that, right?

But I digress. What better time to include a quote from Marilyn Monroe, who once said, "I've often stood silent at a party for hours listening to my movie idols turn into dull and little people." Ah, Marilyn. She makes me wonder about all the people we might consider dull and little, who, if we actively listened to what they have to say, might turn into movie idols right before our eyes.

Active listening is not simply a matter of being passively polite. It's an energetic commitment to paying attention and caring about what other people have to say. Can you think of someone you haven't been actively listening to? Do you think that doing so could change the dynamics of your relationship?

When we hear unexpected, disturbing news, we often shut down. Between shock and an instinct for protective denial, we don't hear much of what we are being told. If it's bad medical news, you may need to have it explained again. Employing active listening skills, which includes taking notes, will do you and everyone around you, a big favor.

---

[5] Legal disclaimer: The author is not intentionally referring to someone he actually knows.

My "Who I Don't Listen to Very Well" List

Who are the people you don't listen to very well? What will you do about it? If you consider yourself an excellent listener, use this space to list the people you think are not listening well enough to you. Write small, because once you get started, that list tends to grow.

Letting Go

"I'm holding on for dear life! Holding on! Just barely holding on!"

Sadly, I'm quoting myself, referring to a night during freshman year of college when I got terribly drunk at a fraternity party and found myself teetering on the edge of a metaphorical cliff, hanging on, so to speak, for dear life. Perhaps I was holding on to the roof, without a metaphor in sight. Yes, I was reeling, slipping downward until all I had to hold on to was the gutter. My friends were leaning out the window, laughing, wondering where I had gone.

"Where are you, you stupid fuck?" they called out affectionately.

"I'm holding on for dear life! Holding on! Just barely holding on!" I cried.

"Well, get your ass back in here, man!" somebody said.

I took those words as great encouragement and managed to crawl to the edge of an open window where I was pulled to safety and a welcome bathroom.

It's a literal example of holding on, thanks to a sturdy gutter. Otherwise, this section might be called Falling Down: The Art of Failure. That's in Part Three; we'll get to that. For now, let's explore the concept of letting go, which can mean so much more than falling off a roof. Here are just a few examples:

- Looking for a way to let go of inhibitions. (Avoid frat houses.)
- Letting go the first time your son leaves home for summer camp.
- Wishing to let go of anger and resentment toward an ex-spouse.
- Secretly letting go of a long-held dream for a promotion at work.
- Imagining through sickness you might be letting go of life, itself.

Can writing help with any of this? I think so. Remember the woman I fell in love with back in Part One? I was trying to let go of her and writing helped. Just the act of physically writing was better than lying around on the couch, feeling miserable and pining for her, although I did my fair share of that, too.

Letting go is hard! It takes practice. Writing takes practice. Meditation takes practice. A crossover dribble takes practice. Playing Bach on a cello takes practice. Real love takes practice.

But back to me. I'm writing this book for you, but also for me. Not just for the cash. Ha ha. As if I'm going to get rich from writing a book—about writing.

But back to me—and letting go, as in letting go of that woman and using writing to do it. Is it working? The jury is still out. Meanwhile, I indulge, which I highly recommend. How's this?

I wanted to write about how much I love her, so I wrote, "Oh, I love her; I love her; I love her so much," and then I felt a little taste of vomit in my mouth, not because of her—because of my bad writing. But I still loved her so I had to keep trying. Until I finally let go.

Gosh, we're all so fragile, and if we're not, we're probably hiding. Some of us hide right inside our own house. Then we have to find our self. I suggest looking in the shower. If you want to discover your own voice, sing in the shower. Pay attention to your voice. Enjoy it. Next time you begin writing, your words will sing more easily.

When—and if— that wears off, put on some music and dance. Pay attention to how you move, from the inside out. That's how you write. Now do it. Get wet and dance. Write. And let go!

I Want to Let Go of _____

I Need to Let Go of _____

I Will Let Go of _____

Dear Cancer

We referred to it back in Part One as the elephant in the room. Earlier in Part Two, Elizabeth Bayer said about cancer: "It's Just a Word." Whether you're a patient, survivor or primary caregiver—be it a spouse, parent, child or sibling—cancer is right there every day, in your face or your rearview mirror.

It needs to be addressed head-on. We can't shy away from it, not for very long. While struggling to deal with it, we need every tool we can fit in the box.

I'm an advocate for communication, both verbal and silent. Writing can be both, depending on whether you choose to read your words out loud.

Part One was about the great big ME in the room. Part Two is about YOU—reaching out to those closest to you: your family, friends and medical team.

But there's one party missing in both of those equations and that is cancer—also known as Dumbo, the elephant in the room we don't often care to acknowledge. What about writing to cancer, literally and in the abstract, because they are practically interchangeable at this point. Consider it an active meditation, a commitment to putting your best foot forward as you work your way through this journey. The cancer does not have to be inside of you in order to write to it. Indirectly, it's inside each of us, especially if there is someone we love currently dealing with a diagnosis.

I hope you'll take a few minutes to reach outside of yourself, and by doing so—by letting go—you will embrace what's right in front of you.

Dear Cancer,

PART THREE

US:
It's All About Us!
(The World at Large)

1 TO DO LIST

2. Write a letter:
   "Dear Cancer"

3.

From You to Us:
So You Want to be a Writer?

For many people, life began when they first held a crayon and scribbled their way into the world. That might've meant drawing on kitchen walls with Magic Markers, tracing images on car windows with sticks or tattooing your legs with ink. Whatever crime your passion may have driven you to commit, it probably made one thing abundantly clear to your parents: you were a precocious child and it would be wise to invest in a large bottle of Mr. Clean.

Some of you may have reached this point later in life and feel a desire to share your thoughts and feelings through writing magazine articles, publishing books or sharing yourself with an endless array of online outlets.

Welcome to Part Three of *Write for Life*. After embracing "me" and focusing on "you" now it's all about reaching out to "us" in whatever form you choose. We'll review some basic tips for effective writing. I stress the word "some" because bookstores and online sites are already overflowing with how-to books on writing. Some of them are wonderful. Some are not. The simple reminders here may help you avoid the burden of a gazillion rules and regulations for what is essentially a straightforward task: telling your story the best way you know how because it may inform and inspire others.

But I'm not a writer! Who cares about my little story?

You're right. The ability to type does not make you a writer. It makes you a typer. But a story resides in your heart, and if you tell it people struggling with similar challenges may benefit.

Do not underestimate your value! While you may not become an overnight sensation, you can find places that will publish your work and some of them may actually pay you, too.

Life changes in an instant. It can happen to any of us. Your story, poem, song or drawing may resonate for someone else in ways you can never imagine. Inside each of us is the potential to heal another through care, compassion and honest communication.

As Soon as I Get a Chance I Want to Write About _____

_____

The Name of My Story Will Be_____

_____

I'll Call My Poem _____

_____

When I Write a Song, I'll Call It _____

_____

Notes for Another Time _____

_____

_____

More Notes_____

_____

Making Art is Like a Three-Way

The French language refers to a sexual tryst with more than two people as a "ménage a trois." In English, I think that's called "good luck." But this book is not *Shades of Grey*. It's *Write for Life*, so let's be optimistic but practical, too. Our three-way concept for making art looks more like a three-legged stool.

Consider this triangular approach: Analytic. Intuitive. Accidental.

You probably already know which word applies to you, especially when it comes to expressing yourself. Do you follow a deliberate path? Do you give yourself permission to feel before you think? Think, then feel? Are you a trustworthy improviser? All of the above?

You know best so follow your strength. No matter which style you favor, all three offer useful perspective. If you tend to analyze things before proceeding, try writing without any pre-conditions. If you are someone who invariably loses track of your intentions, consider outlining an approach before you begin, like you were forced to do in high school or college. Contrary to some opinions, your teachers had the right idea. Finally, if you tend to be an accidental achiever with no apparent plan, consider what happens when you randomly arrive at a great idea. How do you capture it and build it into something?

How do you take any of these three tendencies and turn them into your strength as an artist and communicator? Effective writing is easier when you employ this trio of approaches.

You could return to the preceding page now and fill in some more.

The Hungry Artist

Some say that romance is a lost art. Really? In that case, I volunteer for the debating club, with a special focus on winning the affirmative side of the argument in the aptly titled debate: "Is Romance a Lost Art?"

NO!

Okay, what does this have to do with you—and writing?

The world is ripe for exploration, and if you haven't already found out how deliciously beautiful—and painful—romance can be, now is the time. I, for one, can only hope you've had some experience with it because that means you have already learned about vulnerability—firsthand. Because if there's one state romance will put you in, it's vulnerable. In fact, vulnerable should be the 51st state in our union; it's that much of a sure thing.

Write about your first romance.

Play out a fantasy romance you could see yourself in right now!

Where Should I Write?

I don't know how I made it through high school, sitting at my own individual desk, in the middle of a row of identical desks, with 35 other students surrounding me, each of us daydreaming about the moment we would be liberated from these miniature individualized prisons.

If I lifted my knees quickly and with force, I could make my desk topple backward into the person behind me. If I leaned down fast enough from my chair to pick up a fallen eraser, the twisting motion could make my desk crash into the aisle, with me still in it, causing a domino effect on most surrounding desks. If I tried standing up without first sliding myself out of the one-piece chair and desktop, then all hell could break loose as I'd stagger and fall, setting off a chain reaction of dodging, pushing, yelling, screaming, laughing and copycat-ing. One good piece of adolescent slapstick could disrupt the entire classroom and send me immediately to the principal's office. As undesirable as that might've been considering the principal's tendency to inform my parents, it was also quite convenient because it meant I got to sit outside the principal's office in a normal chair, writing at a real table with ample room to stretch my legs.

Once I got to college, I learned that I could write anywhere, even sprawled out on the grass of the campus quad, breathing in the rarified air of self-importance while flipping frisbees and writing pretentious, romantic poetry.

Now I relish multiple comfort zones for writing, including but not limited to the couch, my bed, the kitchen table, bathrooms, coffee shops, bars, buses, subways, and oh yeah—my desk, where I am right now, slogging away to help you figure out that when it comes to writing, you can do it anywhere.

With so many options, what's a writer to do? Should my desk face the door or the wall? What kind of chair should I use? Maybe my bed can be my office. Should I take the feng shui approach? Do I even know what that means? There are many so good books devoted to coaching writers. I recommend *A WRITER'S SPACE: Make Room to Dream, to Work, to Write* by Eric Maisel, PhD (Adams Media, 2008). Dr. Maisel is widely regarded as America's foremost creativity coach.

Learning to See

Just as a painter observes an apple before he or she begins to paint it as a still life, so too can a writer stare at it in wonder, as if seeing it for the first time. In that moment, doing our best to see an object—or a person—as new, we are invited to express what we see through an open mind.

Try this observation exercise called "The Apple of My Eye."

Take an apple and put it on your kitchen table. Touch it. Smell it. Consider its skin and what's inside it. Then describe it. You may compare the apple to an orange. Then ask: Why do we compare one thing to another? What is a cliché? How can we use comparisons in our writing? What do they illustrate and reveal?

Continue observing the apple. Write a short story of 100 words or a poem or song. Create a one-minute play with the apple as your leading character.

Send one of your creations to five friends. Be somewhat confident of your friendship before sending. Not everyone may be receptive to your ode to a fruit. Depending on the response, consider sending more of your apple writings to others. You'll soon be on your way...

TIP

Verbs come in two forms, active and passive.
Choose active as much as possible.
Please remember:
The adverb is not your friend.

Setting a Scene

The setting of a scene or story is important. For example, what if *The Night Before Christmas* took place in Florida? Santa wouldn't be able to wear a snowsuit or drive a sleigh. The whole holiday season might be quite different.

The location is crucial to a reader's understanding and identification with the content and integral to its narrative. Setting the scene accurately and thoroughly can take a story to the next level. Make it appeal to the five senses. Secure the elements of time. When done well, setting a scene can almost drive the narrative by itself.

What is the setting of your story?

How does your description of that place inform and enhance the story?

Do your descriptive details appeal to the five senses?

How does the setting influence your story?

What happens if you change the location of your story?

Character Description

Can you describe your spouse or best friend?

What do you know about them based on their hair?

Can you describe your doctor?

How would you describe him or her to explain your feelings about them?

Make a list of different characters you could describe from your neighborhood.

Make a second list of specific physical characteristics that describe them.

How do you indicate age, mood, and your feelings toward a person by describing them through specific physical details?

Once you've described a character, can you imagine a story evolving?

More Details

Your kitchen sink is leaking. Should you call a plumber? Think about the plumber who showed up last time. Was he cute? Did he have a you-know-what when he squat down to look under the sink? Does he have a family? Maybe his wife has cancer. Maybe he's getting divorced or trying to stop drinking.

Details. They're everywhere! They surround us, poke, pain, and please us, from morning through daytime and in to the night. Shouldn't we pay attention? If we are mindful of the details in our lives perhaps we will live them more fully.

As a writer, it's your obligation to notice the details, to report them and share with your readers how they make you feel.

Who are your readers? Maybe just you, in a diary for one. Maybe your family, your neighbors or more. It doesn't matter.

Let's imagine you are going to the dry cleaner. Consider all the details of a simple trip you have done numerous times and have come to take for granted. The answers to these questions may trigger a story.

How is your car running?

What do you see on the way to the cleaner—anything new?

Do you have any unfinished business there?

Do you like the person at the counter?

What item are you picking up?

Who gave it to you—someone special—any history?

Who? What? Where? Why? When?

Answer the following questions for yourself or the main character of your story. Creating a "biography" will help you get started.

Who Do You Love?

What Makes You Love Them?

Where Do You Like to Love Them Most?

Why?

When?

Joke Workshop #3

In Part One, you were asked to describe five things that make you laugh. Let's push that a little, keeping in mind that humor has infinite value.

Describe five places where you would be surprised to hear laughter:

1 _____

2 _____

3 _____

4 _____

5 _____

Describe five places where you *need* to hear laughter:

1 _____

2 _____

3 _____

4 _____

5 _____

Same five? Different? Really? How? What do the differences mean? Shall they remain so? Are you sure? Maybe humor belongs where you least expect it.

Beginnings

What provokes a story and makes me want to write? And how do I start? What is my entry point? These are common hurdles, and all too often we overthink our approach to what is essentially a simple story.

Since cancer comes out of the blue, why not take a similar approach when writing about it? Pick one place to start, one idea, one moment in time, and just go for it. Keep it simple. Write about what happened as if you are explaining it to an intimate friend who wasn't there with you.

Each and every one of us reveal a unique piece of the human spirit—from finding strength we never knew to feeling an absolute fear of losing control; from discovering what true support and love means to realizing we are all alone; from finding faith to losing it and finding it again.

Everyone seems to have a story to tell about cancer. Many are uplifting, while others may not be easy to digest. But all are authentic and honest, and they reflect the staggering reality of the cancer world.

The following examples, courtesy of Chicken Soup for the Soul Publishing, are grouped by themes, including diagnosis, breaking the news, a caregiver's reaction, treatment and a doctor's side of the story. You'll see that while each person has a different way of beginning his or her story, in essence they are just talking to us, telling it like it is, as they see and feel. The writing here further demonstrates how personal expression can be a gift—to you, and everyone you know.

THE MOMENT OF DIAGNOSIS

Booger

Out of the blue, I discovered something in my nose. It was bleeding. I went to the doctor. She sent me to the hospital. I filled out the papers and got in line. I stayed overnight. They took a biopsy. I threw up all night. Next morning, they sent me home.

Two weeks later, I went back for the diagnosis and to discuss what form of treatment I would have.

One doctor said, "radiation."

"Hmm," I replied.

"On the right side of your face all the nerves will die and your right eye will drop and your neck will turn blue," he continued.

"Oh really?" I responded.

I decided I needed a second opinion.

The next doctor said, "I think reconstruction is the way to go."

"What's that?" I asked.

"We remove your nose and then we remove the cancer," she began, without blinking an eye. "We pull away the right side of your face, just above the eyelid, over to the left side of your face and the left side then goes back over the right and then we can reconstruct your nose."

"No kidding?" I said. "And you've done this before?"

"All the time," she replied.

I decided I needed a third opinion.

–Bob Lenox

The Brave Spider

"But I'm only twenty-five years old."

"I know."

"I've got two boys to raise by myself."

I sat in Dr. Anderson's office, trying to convince him that I didn't have time for cancer, that I couldn't work it into my schedule and that I simply would not be told that I had it.

"I'm in my twenties, for God's sake," I shouted. "No one my age gets cancer."

Dr. Anderson stood quietly by while I cursed, cried and yelled, and when I didn't have it in me anymore, I collapsed onto his sofa, wishing it were just a bad dream. My mind was racing with the finality of it all.

"Jamie, are you okay?"

Dr. Anderson's voice was smooth and calm. I resented him already.

"Am I okay?" I screeched. " No, I'm not. What am I going to do?"

~Jamie Farris

The Moment

Everybody has a moment when you know nothing is going to be the same ever again, when one part of your life ends and another begins. This is when you know that the changes, for better or worse, are going to be coming hard and fast. You're on a roller coaster and all you can do is hope that your safety belt stays fastened and that you'll come out in one piece. These moments are what make us who we are, and I know I wouldn't be quite me without mine.

Growing up as the oldest of three children in Dwight, Illinois, I had quite an uneventful childhood. My family was a huge part of my life. I had one or two close friends, and that's all I needed. I was healthy. If I had to describe myself, I would say carefree. I laughed a lot. Then came the moment.

~Taylor Gettinger

BREAKING THE NEWS
How Do I Say This?

Dear Parents of Incoming Fourth Graders,
I hope that summer's end finds you well rested and excited to begin a new school year.

Well rested? Who am I kidding? I haven't slept in a week.

I'm really looking forward to getting off to a good start with your kids and I'm very excited to meet with you and your child. But first, I would like to update you on some of the events that have recently transpired in my life and describe how they may affect the experiences of your children at school this year.

What a mouthful. Enough pleasantries, better just say it. IT? Can I say IT without them calling school to withdraw their kids? You're not a serial killer. You're a teacher, and a darn good one, so teach.

I have recently been diagnosed with Stage IV Hodgkin's Lymphoma, a relatively rare cancer of the lymphatic system, discovered after a routine physical this summer. In the coming months, I will be undergoing twelve cycles of ABVD chemotherapy with the possibility of radiation treatment to follow.

Boy, I'd hate to be a parent receiving this letter. Just what a new school year needs—more stress. And what about the kids? I'm sure this isn't how they've pictured their return to the classroom. I can hear it already:

"Watch out! Here he comes! He looks weird! Don't let him touch you!"

And, worst of all, "My grandpa died of cancer. Is my teacher gonna die?"

–Benjamin Schwartz

Cancer Cannot Cripple Love

I was eleven years old when my world came crashing down. It started when my brother tumbled down the stairs, hurting his ankle. We thought he had a sprain, but the tests showed nothing at all. My mom ordered more tests but nobody was worried, especially me. I was more focused on getting ready for my first year of middle school. Surely nothing horrible was happening to my older brother, the one person who has been there for me, as my rock and my friend, from the minute I was born.

I was wrong.

My dad came home from the hospital, sat me down on my bed and looked me straight in the eye. I bounced up and down on the mattress, waiting for him to say Matthew had a sprained ankle. But those weren't the words I heard.

"Emily, Matthew has cancer. Things are going to be different from now on."

~Emily Beaver

FAMILY, FRIENDS & CAREGIVERS

Confessions of a Cancer Caregiver

I am a caregiver who doesn't always love her job.

When my husband, Jim, was diagnosed with lung cancer, I found myself unexpectedly taking care of him. Like many thrust into this situation, I had no prior experience, no medical training, and no proclivity to the position.

I had never taken care of anyone who was seriously ill. I grew up in a home where no one took to his sickbed unless he was near death. Our medicine chest consisted of Mercurochrome, baby aspirin, and a gooey, multi-purpose black salve. We didn't even own a thermometer.

~Cynthia Siegfried

Salutations

Dearest Patient,

I am one of the oncology nurses who treat you, and I would like to offer my perspective of your experience. I'd like to start by commending you on the way you handle yourself through this process. I once had a patient tell me that "cancer was the best thing that ever happened to me." At the time, I didn't understand her statement. However, through years of observation, I can see that cancer truly brings out the best in many people who make the journey.

~Sharon Parkes

TREATMENT

The Room of Hope

The Barcaloungers sit erect with their rigid arms permanently extended, as if in supplication, awaiting the next assortment of chemical bags to be draped upon them. The quiet in the large room seems incongruous to the fear and dread that will soon fill it. Each of the thirty small cubicles is equipped to make a patient comfortable while the fluids trickle slowly down the plastic tubes and into their veins. Muted sounds come from the TVs, distracting the patients as the hours pass slowly by.

The nurses move quickly from station to station, their soft rubber soles squishing on the linoleum. There is a calm to their work, but it still conveys an urgency and efficiency to get each of their patients properly tethered to their respective IV poles. They do this everyday with multiple shifts. It seems like an assembly line but they know that each patient is unique. They possess a gentle touch and soft words, with an expertise that says, "I will get you through this and make it as painless as possible."

~Al Cato

From the Other Side of the Looking Glass

I am an oncologist. When the modern era of bone marrow transplantation (BMT) began in 1968, I was a junior at the Johns Hopkins University School of Medicine in Baltimore, Maryland. Dr. Louis Lasagna, the world-renowned clinical pharmacologist, had guided me there because, in his words, oncology was where the most exciting clinical pharmacology was happening. I dedicated the next eight years of my clinical and scientific training to becoming a member of the Hopkins BMT team. It worked!

But my decision to pursue oncology didn't come easily. I knew that becoming an oncologist meant that I was going to be elbowing death out of the way as best I could and for as long as possible for the rest of my life. And death was going to win the vast majority of the time. Was that the kind of career I wanted to devote my life to?

~Gerald J. Elfenbein

For Chicken Soup for the Soul
submissions guidelines, visit
www.chickensoupforthesoul.com

TIP

If you aspire to write and publish for a general public, then don't write anything before reading Stephen King's TOOLBOX section, pages 101–130 in his book *On Writing* (Pocket Books, 2000). While you're at it, read the whole book.

The Eager Craftsman

By now, you must be inspired to do some kind of writing, and if you haven't already begun, it may be because you don't know which form of writing is best for you. Journaling? Short story? Play? All three? Why not? No rules. Try whatever you feel. Here are some suggested topics for patients, caregivers, and medical professionals:

My Initial Diagnosis
How Do I Deal with My Best Friend's Cancer?
Managing the Strain of Treating Sick People
Learning to Say the "C" Word
Breaking the News to Loved Ones, Friends and Coworkers
What's Happening to My Body?
My Husband Has Cancer: So What About Me?
No-Hair Days (embarrassing and humorous moments)
Cancer and Sexuality
Discovering Faith and Spirituality
Facing Fear and Mortality
Letting Go of a Loved One
What Have I Learned?

The list is endless and ripe for your own twist. While we've covered the idea of journaling, short stories, plays and even letter writing, one thing we've missed is poetry, and since many people favor that craft, let's get to it.

On the next page, you'll have the pleasure of reading a piece by Steve Straight, who sat next to me through four years of English class. I always knew he had an ear to the ground to go with the perpetual smile on his face. Now, while Steve's students are lucky to have him as their teacher, I thank him for sharing his work with all of us.

Encounter in June

Some days the year tries to drag me back
to the cold heart of February

and I lug the word cancer
wherever I go, cancer, which is not a word
but weed, and chooses its own tense.

Some days it is that kind of spring.
But not today.

Today is a day for breathing,
for noticing rhythms too small to be noticed,
like the clattering of tiny toenails on plastic.
Today is this moment kneeling
at the end of a black downspout extension
with my hand held out on the ground, palm up,
breathing slowly and not moving an eyelash;
today is this moment appearing in the black tunnel
a chipmunk, quivering, nosing the great possibility
of faith, of taking the next step directly
into the human, onto the fingers, into the palm—
an island of skin surrounding a black pond of seeds.
Today is the shiny black eyes of the chippy
staring into mine, into the light at the end of the tunnel
that is me.

by Steve Straight
From THE WATER CARRIER
(Curbstone Press, 2002)

Thoughts From Steve

Even though it is many years since I wrote "Encounter in June" following surgery and radiation treatments for cancer, I remember very well the experience of writing it. Kurt Vonnegut once wrote an essay about a teacher he had who said that what artists do is create order out of chaos. This has always made sense to me, and there are few moments in one's life as chaotic as having cancer. All one's typical pillars of normality are gone. One hardly knows what to think, and feelings come randomly and powerfully.

The moment I describe feeding a chipmunk from my hand for the first time was a moment of centering and calm. The concentration of remaining perfectly still while the chipmunk decided if I were friend or threat made every other thought and feeling—all the chaos of that time—disappear. Shortly after the experience, I knew I had to write about it. When I did, I also experienced that calmness, as the focus required to turn experience into art is the same kind of activity. The attention required makes everything else disappear, or at least seem smaller and less important.

I had no thoughts of publishing the poem while I was writing it, and when I write I very rarely do. I write to understand, to explore, and then to help a reader experience what I have.

So my best advice to poets is to avoid statements, especially of theme. The poet's task is not to tell the reader what to think or feel but to describe and narrate so the reader can experience something on his or her own. Simply convey as precisely as you can what you have experienced, and theme will appear naturally.

Thank you Steve.
On the next page, you will encounter a very different sort of poem from a very remarkable young person. She takes the concept of 'I AM' and really runs with it!

I Am a Giant

I am small but big.
I am weak but strong.
Mom took me to the doctors,
Said I have cancer.
Didn't know what it meant,
All I heard was, NO HAIR!
But I was determined to live,
To be who I am today.
A survivor is what I am.
I am a child, a friend, a daughter.
I am five years in remission!
I am a cancer survivor!
WOOHOO!!!!!

by Sarah Smith

A Word on Editing

To pontificate on the art and craft of editing would be pretentious but on the other hand it's absolutely necessary because so much of what is written in the world today is totally unnecessary and takes up a lot of space that could be better used for more productive activities like bowling or raising vegetables in a garden and saving all the trees that are needed to produce paper but that seems like too much even though the people who work in that industry need jobs too to feed and cloth their families and the last thing we need is more unemployment but making a living as a writer is not easy at all and some writers are forced to take logging jobs or work on an assembly line in a paper mill where they may be manufacturing the very paper that could someday be used to print their words in a book that will eventually be read and reviewed and pored over and dissected and edited by a lonely little man or woman in an airless cubicle one idea at a time ruthless but compassionate with an eye for each and every detail making sure they support the overall concept so at the same time little by little page by page comma by comma we can see how necessary and exciting the editing process can be—period.

Less is more, unless it's not (see above). Sometimes less is not enough and you need to speak up and express yourself—more! But after you do, after you fill the page with what feels like perfect splendor; you must kill your darlings. What? That would be murder. That's taking the concept of "blood on the page" to a whole different level, isn't it? "Kill your darlings" means cutting the words, phrases or passages that seem so attractive at the time but in fact, do not advance your story. They may actually impede its progress. Save them for a rainy day.

TIP
WRITE BEFORE YOU EDIT!

Write first. Edit later. Type like a banshee—fast, furious and quixotic, and maybe best of all—rare and romantic. Go for it. Spelling be damned! Grammar and punctuation can wait, too. Go back in later and fix that stuff. Let your fingers do the talking without your head getting in the way.

If You Want to Get Published:
A Writer's To Do List

If you feel pretty sure about what you've written and want to pursue getting published—by blog, magazine article or with a full-blown book—here are a few things to consider.

The Query Letter: A one-page, multipurpose letter to pitch any one of those three. No matter what you're trying to sell, it should include a greeting, a brief description of the book, article or blog you are proposing, why you are qualified to write whatever it is and how you plan on promoting your writing to its appropriate readers.

Imagine you're in an elevator with a literary agent and there's only time for them to read a convincing one-page pitch. That's your query letter.

Next, tell the agent or magazine editor why you are writing to them, in particular. Don't forget contact information, including your email address, a phone number and your website (not a Facebook page!) if you have one. And just in case an agent requests a synopsis, proposal, full manuscript and/or publication history, make sure you have all those documents ready. If you're not sure what these refer to, do your research and determine what you need to learn.

The Competition: Read. Read some more. Whether it's a blog, magazine piece, novella or full-blast book you're aiming for, if you're serious at all about getting published, you must research what's already out there. What makes it work? What's worth emulating—or avoiding?

Process: Once you figure that out, see what you can find out about how that writer got published. If it's a book, check the acknowledgments to see if they thanked their agent. Then look up that agent and find out their submissions guidelines. Many agents include lots of helpful tips on their websites.

After pushing through the business grind of the job, remember to write!

TIP
READ ALOUD!

The Writer and the Need for Meaning

In Part One, Mindy Greenstein, PhD, clinical psychologist, psycho-oncologist and author of *The House on Crash Corner*, spoke about "Why We Write." In her blog, *The Flip Side*, Mindy also discusses the need for meaning in what we write.

I transformed the way I experienced my own crisis—cancer—when I turned it into material for my writing. The pain of dealing with my initial doctors, for instance, was now excellent material for teaching future doctors not to behave the same way. I'd long known I wanted to write about my experiences as a psycho-oncologist. Now, I had much more to offer. And I knew I wasn't going to stop until it got published because I had a goal that meant too much to me to do otherwise. If it didn't happen, it would not be for lack of trying.

Psychologists Jerome Bruner and Henri Zukier suggest that our minds have two ways of taking in the world. When we perceive the world in paradigmatic mode, we act like scientists, connecting facts, patterns and universal principles through which we categorize and understand our environment. The narrative mode, on the other hand, is what allows us to endow life with meaning through the stories we tell about it. We note intentions and goals, beginnings, middles and ends. And if the story I told about my cancer was that it would help me be better at my profession, and force me to write the book I'd always wanted to write, or make me appreciate my friends and family as never before, then my experience of the cancer itself became more tolerable. Sometimes, it was even funny.

This isn't a new idea. Writers are famous for turning their suffering into material. They share their vision with others, who might learn from what they read. Or they might be encouraged to think back on their own lives and create their own coherent stories. Or they might learn, simply by being reminded that they matter, just as the characters and events in the books they read matter.

Writers create a sense of community in the people who read them, and these communities that writing creates—between reader and writer, or between readers and other readers—transcend time and place.

The Myth of Writer's Block

There is no such thing as writers block. If you get stuck, if you don't know what to write, then your heart and mind are probably not in the right place at that very minute. Like a computer, you may simply need to reboot.

A bit of mindfulness should do the trick. With traditional mindfulness, your central goal is to be in the moment. For example, when you eat a potato, you really eat that particular potato. You're not eating an entire field of potatoes. You're not thinking about the Irish potato famine of 1845. You're being present with that one potato, paying attention to each bite, to its taste and texture, and to the nourishment and enjoyment that potato is providing. On the other hand, creative mindfulness occurs when you eat that potato and work on your novel at the same time. This type of creativity can also be achieved with other foods.

All kidding aside, being a writer is not about writing. That's what you do when you compose an email. Writing is a tool for self-discovery, effective communication and storytelling.

Being a writer means you are willing to fearlessly explore your own thoughts and feelings. By doing so, you liberate neurons in your brain, effectively emptying your mind and preparing yourself for creating. This may yield an explosion of inventiveness or the equivalent of a quiet walk in the park. Personality and circumstance dictate much of that.

If you are still struggling, make a list of the issues that seem to be preventing you from writing. Be open and give issues a chance to surface.

For those dealing with disease, divorce, drugs, or anything throwing a huge monkey wrench into life, then cleansing—physically and spiritually—is key to getting better. Writing may provide the personal leverage needed for change.

Choosing Fun Over Fear and Peace Over Pain

Stephen King says, "Writing isn't about making money, getting famous, getting dates, getting laid, or making friends. In the end, it's about enriching the lives of those who will read your work, and enriching your own life, as well. It's about getting up, getting well, and getting over."

What more can I add? One more thought from the master, himself:

"Writing is magic, as much the water of life as any other creative art. The water is free. So drink. Drink and be filled up."

Open your heart. In the moment, as resources allow, you can designate your mindset and point your heart in the direction you choose. Writing can help you do that, bringing you closer to your own center and the people you love.

For every author, professional and amateur, personal expression can be a gift. That's what this book is all about.

Welcome to *Write for Life*. I hope it's working for you.

WRITE FOR LIFE

Acknowledgments

I've met many people contributing great things in the fight against cancer. They educate and inspire me. Their encouragement has led me to create this book.

I begin with Elizabeth Bayer, who taught me about coping with change, communicating with loved ones and doctors, and ultimately, how to embrace fate. Fortunately, Chicken Soup for the Soul Publishing included Elizabeth's memoir, *It's Just a Word,* as an added feature of *The Cancer Book.* Thank you, Amy Newmark, for supporting Elizabeth and that entire project.

It's impossible to acknowledge each of the men, women and children who enriched our lives with their stories, but I owe them my gratitude for letting me into their lives. Sadly, we have lost some of these people, and I would like to extend my best wishes to their families.

The Cancer Book led to an invitation from Genentech, Inc., to conduct "Write to Fight Cancer" workshops in hospitals around the country. Thanks to Genentech, Mai-Lise Nguyen and her wonderful colleagues at Weber Shandwick, I had the chance to develop some of the material presented here.

Altos Solutions and See Your Chart have also played a role in supporting this book. I look forward to our continuing partnership.

A special thanks to Flash Rosenberg for her friendship as well as her artwork, which visually defines *Write for Life.*

To have Linda Roberts's blessing is my good fortune.

James P. Walsh is a savvy editor. Bruce Kluger is Bruce Kluger and I thank him for that (and the cover).

Thanks to Mercy Ameyaw for designing www.writeforlife.info. She maintains the site while serving as the U.S. Army's most beautiful soldier in Afghanistan.

Speaking of secret ops, others may not realize their role in making this book happen. They include Mark Banschick, Edel Blumberg, Marlo Thomas, Debbie Wasserman-Schultz and Hillary Clinton. Thanks to each of you.

And to my children, Max and Stella: the ways you move me have never been a secret.

Resources

The organizations listed here are just a few of the many informative and inspirational online resources for anyone affected by a cancer diagnosis.

calmcancercounseling.com
Helps individuals transform cancer challenges into successful solutions.

Cancer Support Community
Free counseling, support groups, education and financial assistance.
www.cancersupportcommunity.org

CancerCare
Free, professional support services for anyone affected by cancer.
www.cancercare.org

CaringBridge
Free, private websites connecting patients to their loved ones.
www.caringbridge.org

CarePages
Online community of personalized websites and blogs.
www.carepages.com

MyLifeLine
Free, personalized websites for cancer patients, survivors and caregivers.
www.mylifeline.org

IHadCancer.com
User-friendly site, international social support network bringing together survivors, fighters, and those newly diagnosed, along with caregivers, colleagues, friends and families.

Imerman Angels

Founded in 2003 by cancer survivor Jonny Imerman, matches a person newly touched by cancer with someone who has survived the same type of cancer (a Mentor Angel). Free matches also provided for caregivers.

www.imermanangels.org

Stupid Cancer

Empowers young adults affected by cancer through innovative and award-winning programs and services. A bullhorn for the young adult cancer movement.

www.stupidcancer.org

Recommended Reading

Articles/Journals

From *The Oncologist*, February 2008

"Expressive Writing Appears to Change
Thoughts and Feelings About Cancer"

*STUDY SUGGESTS A SINGLE 20-MINUTE WRITING SESSION
POSITIVELY IMPACTS A PATIENT'S QUALITY OF LIFE*

Expressive writing—writing about one's deepest thoughts and feeling—may help change the way cancer patients think and feel about their disease. In one of the first studies published in an oncology journal about the benefits of writing therapy, researchers say those who immediately reported changes in thoughts about their illness also reported a better physical quality of life three weeks later.

"Previous research suggests expressive writing may enhance physical and psychological well-being," said Nancy P. Morgan, MA, writing clinician and director of the Lombardi Comprehensive Cancer Center's Arts & Humanities Program. "But most of those studies involved three to five writing sessions that were conducted in a controlled laboratory setting. Here, we found that just one writing session in a busy cancer clinic where the patients are frequently interrupted can still have a positive impact on patients."

"Waiting for your appointment can be a time of anxiety and stress for cancer patients," said Bruce D. Cheson, MD, head of hematology at Lombardi and a coauthor on the study. "I'm pleased to see that so many of our patients were interested in this kind of therapy. Our study supports the benefit of an expressive writing program and the ability to integrate such a program into a busy clinic."

From *Coping® with Cancer,* March/April 2009

By Nancy Morgan

Twenty years of research in controlled laboratory settings indicates writing may contribute to improved physical and emotional health. Our study moved research from the lab to the waiting room of a busy cancer clinic. We invited people with leukemia and lymphoma in our hospital waiting room to participate in the study. Participants completed surveys and responded to the question, "How has cancer changed you, and how do you feel about those changes?"

Study results suggest there may be a link between those who felt writing changed the way they thought about their cancer and an improved physical quality of life (reported weeks later in a follow up interview). Most participants described a pattern of emotional change during their cancer experience, starting with the shock of diagnosis, then moving to acceptance, gratitude, and descriptions of life improvements in the areas of family, self-care, spirituality, and work.

As one participant wrote, "I don't like to talk about the cancer even though I feel like I should. Writing helps to get the feelings out of me."

Whether you use writing to take a break from cancer or to confront cancer directly, writing becomes a surprisingly effective tool for self-expression and simply feeling better.

Nancy Morgan is a writing clinician and director of the Arts and Humanities program at Lombardi Comprehensive Cancer Center at Georgetown University in Washington, D.C.

"Writing about emotions may ease stress and trauma"

Stress, trauma, and unexpected life developments—such as a cancer diagnosis, a car accident, or a layoff—can throw people off stride emotionally and mentally. Writing about thoughts and feelings that arise from a traumatic or stressful life experience—called expressive writing—may help some people cope with the emotional fallout of such events. But it's not a cure-all, and it won't work for everyone. Expressive writing appears to be more effective for people who are not also struggling with ongoing or severe mental health challenges, such as major depression or post-traumatic stress disorder.

Dr. James W. Pennebaker, currently chair of the psychology department at the University of Texas, Austin, has conducted much of the research on the health benefits of expressive writing.

The act of thinking about an experience, as well as expressing emotions, seems to be important. In this way, writing helps people to organize thoughts and give meaning to a traumatic experience. The process of writing may enable them to better regulate their emotions. It's also possible that writing about something fosters an intellectual process— he act of constructing a story about a traumatic event—that helps someone break free of the endless mental cycling more typical of brooding or rumination.

Finally, when people open up privately about a traumatic event, they are more likely to talk with others about it—suggesting that writing leads indirectly to reaching out for social support that can aid healing. Even with these caveats, however, expressive writing is such an easy, low-cost technique—much like taking a good brisk walk—that it may be worth trying.

Books

A Survivor's Guide to Kicking Cancer's Ass
Dena Mendes
Hay House, Inc., 2011

A Walk Between Heaven and Earth
Burghild Nina Holzer
Bell Tower, 1994

Crazy Sexy Cancer Survivor
Kris Carr
skirt!, 2008

8 Minute Meditation
Victor Davich
A Perigee Book, 2004

Journal to the Self
Twenty-two Paths to Personal Growth
Kathleen Adams, MA
Warner Books, Inc., 1990

Life, with Cancer: The Lauren Terrazzano Story
Frank Terrazzano & Paul Lonardo
Health Communications, Inc., 2012

One Year to a Writing Life:
Twelve Lessons to Deepen Every Writer's Craft
Susan M. Tiberghien
Da Capo Press, 2007

On Writing Well
William Zinsser
Harper, 1998

Our Cancer Year
Harvey Pekar and Joyce Brabner
Art by Frank Stack
Four Walls Eight Windows, 1994

Slipping Reality
Emily Beaver
Author House, 2012

The Places That Scare You
A Guide to Fearlessness in Difficult Times
Pema Chödron
Shambhala Classics, 2002

We're In This Together: A Caregiver's Story
Rob Harris
Visual Impressions Publishing, 2012

Writing Down the Bones
Freeing the Writer Within
Natalie Goldberg
Shambhala, 2005

About the Author

David Tabatsky is a writer, editor, teacher, director and performing artist. He received his BA in Communications and an MA in Theatre Education, both from Adelphi University.

David is the coauthor of *The Cancer Book: 101 Stories of Courage, Support and Love* and editor of Elizabeth Bayer's *It's Just a Word,* both published by Chicken Soup for the Soul Publishing in 2009. He is the coauthor, with Bruce Kluger, of *Dear President Obama: Letters of Hope from Children Across America* also published in 2009. David wrote *The Boy Behind the Door: How Salomon Kool Escaped the Nazis* (2009). With Dr. Mark Banschick, David coauthored The *Intelligent Divorce*—Books One and Two (2009 and 2010) and *The Wright Choice: Your Family's Guide to Healthy Eating, Modern Fitness and Saving Money (2011),* with Dr. Randy Wright. David was the consulting editor for Marlo Thomas and her *New York Times* bestseller *The Right Words at the Right Time, Volume 2: Your Turn* (2006). He has published two editions of *What's Cool Berlin* a comic travel guide to Germany's capital, and has written for The Forward, Parenting and Sesame Street Parent, among others.

David has worked professionally in theatre and circus as an actor, clown and juggler, at New York City's Lincoln Center, Radio City Music Hall and the Beacon Theatre and throughout the United States and Europe, most notably at the Chamäleon in Berlin, New End Theatre in London, Folies Pigalle in Paris and the Edinburgh Fringe Festival, where *THE STAGE* wrote, "He is a supremely skillful performer and a fine actor, reaching levels no other comics have matched at this Fringe." David also directed Kinderzirkus Taborka at the renowned Tempodrom in Berlin.

David has taught for the American School of London, die Etage in Berlin, the Big Apple Circus School, The United Nations International School and the Cathedral of St. John the Divine. He served on the theatre faculty at Adelphi University and The Cooper Union and as a teaching artist for The Henry Street Settlement with a focus on special education. He teaches circus arts at Sunrise Day Camp, America's only dedicated day camp for children with cancer and their siblings.

Please visit www.tabatsky.com and www.writeforlife.info.

Please visit

www.writeforlife.info

Contact

David Tabatsky

david@tabatsky.com

Made in the USA
Charleston, SC
16 September 2014